Rich Grace in Poor Soil le̟
For anyone who feels bru
will refresh the soul. Written with a sharpness of insight and a
flair for illustration, *Rich Grace in Poor Soil* is a tonic. Having
been present for most of the Thursday mornings where these
chapters found their original setting, I am delighted that these
studies will now find a wider and more permanent audience. A
marvelous achievement.

Derek W. H. Thomas
Senior Minister, First Presbyterian Church, Columbia,
South Carolina
Chancellor's Professor, Reformed Theological Seminary
Teaching Fellow, Ligonier Ministries

Ken Wingate wants you to wallow in grace. In this manual
for the Christian life, he writes of deep grace with such a light
touch—and good sense. Insights abound; the book is simply
fun to read.

Dale Ralph Davis
Respected Author and Old Testament Scholar

Christians delight to read about grace in the way that happy
families pore over old holiday photographs. In this book, Ken
Wingate uses the Biblical image of a vineyard to unpack grace
in its various and diverse aspects in a way that is both simple
and profound. This is warm nourishment for the soul.

Iain Duguid
Professor of Old Testament, Westminster Theological Seminary,
Philadelphia, Pennsylvania

One of the most frequently used metaphors in the Bible to
picture the Christian life is that of the vineyard producing

fruit. Kenneth Wingate has done an excellent job drawing upon this rich imagery to convey the clear teaching of Scripture concerning our growing in grace. Easy to understand, yet challenging to live, this book will be a great help to your pursuit of personal holiness. May God use it to bring forth much fruit in your life.

Steven J. Lawson
President, OnePassion Ministries
Teaching Fellow, Ligonier Ministries
Professor, The Master's Seminary
Lead Preacher, Trinity Bible Church of Dallas

Ken Wingate's *Rich Grace in Poor Soil* vividly explores the Bible's 'vineyard' theology as a study in God's wonderful, sovereign grace. Engaging and encouraging, this book digs into the deep soil of divine grace to display wonders that will lead its readers into praise. Filled with illuminating stories and illustrations, Wingate's book is itself a planting of the Lord that will bear rich fruit in the lives of those who read. If you are looking to grow spiritually and enlarge your understanding of God's marvellous ways, this is the book for you!

Richard D. Phillips
Senior Minister, Second Presbyterian Church of Greenville, South Carolina

Rich Grace
IN POOR SOIL

Rich Grace
IN POOR SOIL

GROWING IN THE MASTER'S GRIP
Kenneth B. Wingate

CHRISTIAN
FOCUS

Copyright © Kenneth B. Wingate 2022

Paperback ISBN 978-1-5271-0806-6
Ebook ISBN 978-1-5271-0882-0

10 9 8 7 6 5 4 3 2 1

Published in 2022
by
Christian Focus Publications Ltd,
Geanies House, Fearn, Ross-shire,
IV20 1TW, United Kingdom.

www.christianfocus.com

Cover design by Pete Barnsley

Drawings at the end of each chapter are by Miriam Wingate Ashworth.

Printed and bound by
Bell & Bain, Glasgow

CONTENTS

FOREWORD

Were you a stranger wandering around city centre Columbia, South Carolina, and found yourself in Lady Street looking a little lost you might be greeted by a man walking purposefully in the opposite direction. If the stranger paused, asked politely if he could help in any way, and then gave you clear and specific directions to your intended destination, or information about the city and its history, or things in it that might be of interest, the chances are you would have just met Ken Wingate. If perchance you were looking for the offices in which he and his colleagues practise law, then you would also have met the managing partner. If you were an educator, you would be speaking to someone who had served as the chair of the State of South Carolina Commission on Higher Education. If finance was your interest you have encountered a past Treasurer for the

State of South Carolina. If your concerns were in the area of job development, you would now be talking to a former member of the South Carolina Jobs-Economic Development Authority. If you happened to need estate planning, this is his specialty. And if you were admiring the church buildings that impressed you as you turned the corner from Marion Street into Lady Street, he would probably take the opportunity to lead the conversation round from the buildings to the living church that meets there and which he has faithfully served as an elder. And yes, in an extended conversation you might discover that he is a devoted husband, father, and grandfather. One thing he would not tell you is that he is also the holder of the highest civilian honour that can be awarded in this his home state, The Order of the Palmetto. Now you know that too!

But if you were a Christian, and a reader, you might even wonder if this could possibly be the Ken Wingate whose name you have noticed on one or other of the books he has written. But, you would probably dismiss the thought on the grounds that there must be more than one Ken Wingate. There probably are, but *this* Ken Wingate, servant of the law and servant of his Lord, his family, his church, his state, and his city is also *that* Ken Wingate! And as one of his friends I have the privilege of introducing him and his new book.

In these pages you will find hints of Ken Wingate's many interests and commitments. But what has taken me by surprise is the extent to which they reveal a city lawyer who also has a deep love for, knowledge of, and a commitment to the agrarian world. And as I would expect of my friend, following in the footsteps of his Master, he has put this to good spiritual use. And so, if you are a city dweller you will probably find yourself discovering new things about nature – but in order that you may learn lessons about grace. Here the eyes that have been trained to notice details as they pore over legal documents have also been trained spiritually by God's Word, and inspired by Christ's own example, to see that since we live in God's creation we should learn to see his hand revealed in all his handiwork. The sixteenth century reformer John Calvin--who also, incidentally, trained in the law--loved to describe the created world as the theatre of God's glory. As he also enjoyed saying, in bringing creation into being it was as if God was putting on his outside clothing to appear in public. Ken Wingate continues that great tradition of lawyers!

When we come to Christ as Saviour we discover an unexpected bonus: the Saviour is also the Creator. As John tells us in the Prologue to his Gospel, the Word that was made flesh is also the one through whom all things were made. And so, when Christ is known,

> Something lives in every hue,
> Christless eyes have never seen.
> (Henry Francis Lyte)

The Lord Jesus saw this with unclouded vision. The Gospels are full of birds and flowers, trees and bushes, fields and crops, as well as farmers and harvests, and of course a vine and a Vinedresser. And in *Rich Grace in Poor Soil* Ken Wingate lends us his eyes as he reflects on lessons he himself has learned in the countryside--lessons that all of us, no matter where we live, can apply to our own lives. One of his earlier books is called *A Father's Gift*. This one might well be sub-titled *A Farmer's Gift*. I hope you enjoy it and benefit from it!

Sinclair B. Ferguson
October 2021

To the 'Thursday Men's Bible Fellowship' in Columbia, South Carolina.

Be strengthened by the grace that is in Christ Jesus.

AUTHOR'S PREFACE

My life as a weekend farmer and gamekeeper began in the 1980s. The family farm near Charleston, South Carolina, called 'Limerick,' is the remnant of an old Lowcountry plantation, dating to 1707. Lying on the east branch of the Cooper River, near the Atlantic Ocean, Limerick is blessed with mild winters, long summers, and a lot of moisture. In centuries past, its dark soil produced timber, rice, indigo and cotton. Today, we grow pine trees, with crops for the wildlife and livestock, plus figs and grapes for the humans. But my sentimental favorite, by far, is the grapes.

Down the lane at the arbor, between the soybean field and a pine grove, are two rows of grape vines – the humble, Southern varieties we call muscadines (purple-skinned) and scuppernongs (bronze-skinned). There is something romantic in the arched vines, the lush foliage, and the succulent fruit. A vineyard is a portrait of beauty and grace, proclaiming the Creator's kindness and creativity. It is a spiritual experience to grow grapes!

The careful observer, however, finds a mystery in the vineyard. How can heavy clusters of fruit grow at the end of long, flimsy branches? Do the vines defy gravity? The riddle is solved by a closer look at the plant. Beneath the leaves, the vine's tendrils tenaciously grip the arbor. The botanical definition of a tendril is 'a threadlike organ of climbing plants, which twines around some other body, to support the plant.'

Without support, climbing plants could not grow, blossom, and bear fruit. Branches lying on the ground would not thrive, lacking air circulation and exposure to light. Any fruit would be easy prey for pests. Tendrils are essential for the plant's life support.

Tendrils are a magnificent display of divine bioengineering. They are:

- Silent – they have no leaves, and make no show.
- Supple – they are flexible and bend easily, to find the right grip.
- Secure – once in place, they never let go.
- Smart – they wrap around and around, of their own initiative.
- Specialized – they serve only one purpose.
- Sovereign – they determine the direction of the plant's growth.
- Symbolic – they show the intricate design of the Creator.

That is the picture of grace! Grace is God's supernatural work in growing and sustaining the Christian believer. His transforming grace produces succulent, eternal fruit in the lives of all His people. Every believer attached to Christ bears fruit by His grace.

'Grace' is a common word in Scripture, appearing over 200 times. But its power is veiled by its stealth, and its progress is belied by its slow growth. The root definition of grace is 'unmerited favor.' But it is also far more. The initiating grace of the One who bestows it also stimulates a responsive grace in the one who receives it. John Owen, the seventeenth-century theologian, called this 'purchased grace.' Grace *(unmerited favor)* supplies grace *(transforming power)* to produce grace *(genuine Christlikeness)*. Grace is the life of God at work in the soul of man!

The growth of grace follows the same pattern as the germination and growth of a seed. To explain it, Scripture uses metaphors from nature. Grace is compared to a seed, a grain, a vine, and a tree. Each stage of spiritual life follows the natural pattern: 'first the blade, then the ear, then the full grain in the ear' (Mark 4:28). Grace is the miraculous work of God, infusing spiritual life into human seedlings, 'that they may be called oaks of righteousness, a planting of the LORD, that he may be glorified' (Isa. 61:3).

The gospel of grace is the divine, collaborative work of all three persons of the Trinity. Though mankind has been ruined by the fall, by grace we are regenerated by the Spirit, redeemed by the Son, and reconciled to the Father.

The natural world proves that cultivating crops requires many 'inputs' – time, material and labor. But the investment is worth it for the harvest. So the gospel reveals the extraordinary price our Father paid to insure a rich harvest. If He did not spare His own Son, but freely gave Him up for us all, will He not also with Him graciously give us all things? The power of His irresistible and all-sufficient grace will never let us go.

Well, let's step into the vineyard.

Ken Wingate
Columbia, South Carolina
October 2021

1

THE VINEYARD

'I am the true vine, and my Father is the vinedresser'
(John 15:1).

In the early 2000s, John and Molly Chester dropped out of the corporate rat race to pursue a new life. Leaving other careers, they purchased 200 acres of barren land in Moorpark, California, and euphemistically named it 'Apricot Lane Farms.' Thus began a seven-year battle to establish an organic apricot farm in an industrial wasteland. Their epic struggle against pests, predators, and wildfires was chronicled in the award-winning documentary, *The Biggest Little Farm* (Neon Films, 2018). A film critic extolled, 'Mother Nature has never been more inspiring!'

That film critic was partly right and partly wrong. There is no such thing as 'Mother Nature.' There is a living God who created the heavens and the earth. But the work He is doing is indeed inspiring. And, like the movie, the story of His recreation (the story of grace) unfolds in a garden. It may not look like much now, but wait until it is restored!

THIS WORLD IS A VINEYARD

The inspired, inerrant Word of God features gardens, both literal and figurative, beginning in Genesis and ending in Revelation. When God created the heavens and the earth, He filled the world with living creatures and made mankind in His image. Then it says:

> And the LORD God planted a garden in Eden, in the east, and there he put the man whom he had formed. And out of the ground the LORD God made to spring up every tree that is pleasant to the sight and good for food. The tree of life was in the midst of the garden, and tree of the knowledge of good and evil (Gen. 2:8-9).

His garden was beautiful and lush.

But the sanctity of the garden was spoiled when Adam and Eve disobeyed God, taking and tasting the forbidden fruit of the tree of the knowledge of good and evil. When the Lord visited the garden in the cool of the day, Adam and Eve fled from Him, aware of their nakedness and filled with shame. The Lord had come to commune with Adam and Eve, as if to inquire, 'What have you done today to exercise dominion over the garden?' But their fellowship had turned to fear. Their oneness with God, each other, and the ground itself was forever changed.

Yet even the curse on their disobedience contained, from the moment it was pronounced, the seeds of God's grace in His plan to restore all things to its original design. The 'covenant of grace' began with God's promise to send a redeemer to destroy the works of the serpent. 'I will put enmity between you and the woman, and between your offspring and her offspring; he shall bruise your head, and you shall bruise his heel' (Gen. 3:15).

Though the Lord's garden has been marred by man's sin, bearing the scars of sickness and death, pestilence and destruction, conflict and warfare, God's plan of redemption is to reverse the effects of the Fall. 'Thus says the LORD God: 'On the day that I cleanse you from all your iniquities … they shall say, "This land that was desolate has become like the garden of Eden"' (Ezek. 36: 33, 35). Operation Grace has begun!

The world as we know it will one day be fully restored as a garden, in 'the new heaven and the new earth' (Rev. 21:1). 'He will wipe away every tear from their eyes, and death will be no more, neither shall there be mourning, nor crying, nor pain anymore … Behold, I am making all things new' (Rev. 21:4-5). The river of life will flow through the garden, and on its banks will be the tree of life, whose leaves are for the healing of the nations. No longer will there be the curse of separation from God, but face-to-face fellowship with God and His Son will be restored. The final words of the Bible are this sure promise: 'The grace of the Lord Jesus be with all' (Rev. 22:21). In other words, by His grace the restoration will be complete.

The story of redemption – 'HIS-story' – is really the story of grace. Redemption is the outworking of His undeserved favor, finding its fulfillment in the kingdom of grace. Human history begins and ends in a garden.

THE VINEYARD BELONGS TO OUR FATHER

One of the first questions we ask when we see a manicured property is, 'Who owns this place?' We understand that the grandeur of a landscape reflects the deep care and abundant resources of its owner. To see a beautiful lawn framed by blooming flowers and manicured hedges, or a tree-lined avenue with orderly stone walls and freshly painted gates, tells us the owner cares.

Some may look at the world and see only the ravages of disease, distress, and disorder, concluding there is no master, or at least not one who is powerful and good. The atheist and the cynic alike pronounce, 'There is no God.' But only a fool looks at the universe and concludes there is no God. His eternal power and divine nature can be clearly perceived in all that has been made. The hymn writer William Cowper saw life with eyes of faith when he wrote, 'Blind unbelief is sure to err, and scan his work in vain. God is his own interpreter, and he will make it plain.'[1]

William Cowper's pastor and friend, John Newton, penned the best-known hymn in the English language, 'Amazing Grace.' Newton's major theme in life was the animating and sustaining power of God's sovereign grace in this world:

> We cannot watch, unless he watches with us; we cannot strive, unless he strives with us; we cannot stand one moment, unless he holds us up; and we believe we must perish after all, unless his faithfulness is engaged to keep us. But this we trust he will do, not for our righteousness, but for his own name's sake, and because having loved us with an everlasting love, he has been pleased in loving kindness to draw us to himself, and to be found of us when we sought him not.[2]

The early Christians knew exactly who owns and rules this world. When they felt pressure from persecuting enemies, they boldly cried out to the 'Sovereign Lord, who made the heavens

---

1. 'God Moves In A Mysterious Way,' *Olney Hymns in Three Books*, Chiswick, 1818, p. 199.
2. John Newton, *Select Letters of John Newton*, The Banner of Truth Trust, 2011, p. 81.

and the earth and the sea and everything in them,' and asked Him to 'do whatever your hand and your plan had predestined to take place' (Acts 4:24, 29). Never think for a moment that a seemingly chaotic world means that God is not in control. He plants His footsteps in the sea, and rides upon the storm.

THE LORD IS RESTORING HIS GARDEN

Every garden begins with a designer's plan. The Lord's master plan for His people was declared long ago by His prophets. He 'had a vineyard on a very fertile hill. He dug it and cleared it of stones, and planted it with choice vines; he built a watchtower in the midst of it, and hewed out a wine vat in it; and he looked for it to yield grapes' (Isa. 5:1-2). Jesus would pick up this same theme in a parable to explain the redemptive nature of His work:

> There was a master of a house who planted a vineyard and put a fence around it and dug a winepress in it and built a tower and leased it to tenants, and went into a far country. When the season for fruit drew near, he sent his servants to the tenants to get his fruit (Matt. 21:33-34).

The point of these passages is two-fold. First, the Lord loves His vineyard. He loves the plants, nurtures the fruit, and expects a full harvest. As a garden causes what is sown in it to sprout up, so the Lord God will cause righteousness and praise to sprout up among the nations (Isa. 61:11). This is what He cares about the most in the world. Second, the Lord has done everything necessary to insure that growth happens. Left untended, the vineyard would yield only wild grapes. Therefore, He commits the resources to produce a bumper crop of sweet fruit. And, as any farmer can attest, the task is far more difficult and expensive than we imagine!

God is like that farmer. The personal cost to Him is staggering. 'He who did not spare his own son, but gave him up for us all, how will he not also with him graciously give us all things?' (Rom. 8:32). He gives *graciously*, generously committing all the resources needed to bear fruit.

From God's perspective, the grand design of human history is to set apart a people for His own possession. At the heart of the covenant of grace is divine relationship: 'I will be their God, and they will be my people' (Jer. 31:33).

From the believer's perspective, our chief aim in life is to grow in grace, bearing fruit for God's glory. But how can the mortal put on immortality, the rebel be reconciled to the King?

THE LORD'S INSTRUMENT IS CHRIST

One day, Jesus was teaching in the synagogue, and He asked for the scroll of Isaiah's prophecy to be brought to Him. Finding the text, He read,

> The Spirit of the Lord is upon me, because he has anointed me to proclaim good news to the poor. He has sent me to proclaim liberty to the captives and recovering of sight to the blind, to set at liberty those who are oppressed, to proclaim the year of the Lord's favor (Luke 4:18-19).

When He finished reading, the eyes of all in the synagogue were fixed on Him, and He said, 'Today this Scripture has been fulfilled in your hearing.' You could have heard a pin drop. He claimed to be the instrument through which *the Lord's favor* – did you catch those words? – would be administered. The kingdom of grace had arrived! Jesus is the king of grace, the liberator of the captives, the healer of the blind, the herald of the good news of God's favor.

This is the key to understanding grace. Without Jesus, the source of grace, there is no access to God's favor. With Jesus, we stand in God's grace. 'We have peace with God through our Lord Jesus Christ. Through him we have also obtained access by faith into this grace in which we stand' (Rom. 5:1-2). Jesus gives us right standing with God, and allows us to tap into His endless supply of grace.

The Apostle Paul was a champion of the gospel of free grace. In his letter to the Roman believers, Paul explains that all have sinned (Rom. 5:12) and therefore deserve death. 'But God shows his love for us in that while we were still sinners, Christ died for us' (5:8). Therefore, 'we were reconciled to God by the death of his Son' and 'shall be saved by his life' (5:10). 'The free gift by the grace of that one man Jesus Christ abounded for many … much more will those who receive the abundance of grace and the free gift of righteousness reign in life through the one man Jesus Christ' (5:15, 17).

The substitutionary death of Jesus is why the acrostic 'G.R.A.C.E.' is often cited– 'God's Riches At Christ's Expense.' Though that expression may sound trite, it drives home the point that Christ is the instrument of God's grace toward us: 'For you know the grace of our Lord Jesus Christ, that though he was rich, yet for your sake he became poor, so that you by his poverty might become rich' (2 Cor. 8:9). Elsewhere, Paul put it this way: 'In [Christ] we have redemption through his blood, the forgiveness of our trespasses, according to the riches of his grace' (Eph. 1:7). Jesus alone is the fountain of grace.

Jesus lives and reigns, laboring on behalf of His people without ceasing. As one commentator put it, 'We are in his thoughts and prayers every day, and he is working with every ounce of his being to restore us from our sad exile to the glory to which we are entitled by the grace of God.'[3]

---

3. Philip G. Ryken, *Exodus: Saved for God's Glory,* Crossway, 2005, p. 377.

GRACE IS A RELATIONSHIP WITH JESUS

As Southerners, we hear the word 'grace' used often in daily conversation. It creeps into our lexicon in various ways, mostly as offshoots of its true meaning. It is a popular name for women: 'Grace.' It is a description of a good athlete: 'he moves with grace.' We use it to describe a friendly or welcoming attitude: 'Bless her heart, she is such a gracious hostess.' It is even a colloquialism for the prayer before a meal: 'John Henry, will you say grace?' There are hints of true grace in these phrases, but its root meaning is obscured.

Grace is not a *thing*, like a food supplement, that makes us bigger and stronger. It is the influence of a personal relationship that changes how we think and how we act. Just as a spouse or close friend slowly and imperceptibly affects the way we think, speak and act, so it is with the living Christ. 'The Word became flesh and dwelt among us, and we have seen his glory, glory as of the only Son from the Father, full of grace and truth … And from his fullness we have all received, grace upon grace' (John 1:14, 16). Simply knowing Jesus is the life-giving, life-changing agent that brings us into fellowship with God and fundamentally changes everything about us. The Father of grace produces children of grace. Grace is not a thing, but a relationship!

John Winthrop, the English lawyer who became leader of the Massachusetts Bay Colony in New England in 1630, described his relationship with Jesus this way:

> I have now grown familiar with the Lord Jesus Christ … If I go abroad, he goes with me; when I return he comes home with me; I talk to him along the way; he lies down with me, and usually I awake with him; and so sweet is his love to me, I desire nothing but him in heaven or earth.[4]

---

4. Ibid., p. 1024.

24

The dynamic power of Christ's indestructible life becomes the lifeline for His people. 'I am the vine; you are the branches. Whoever abides in me and I in him, he it is that bears much fruit, for apart from me you can do nothing' (John 15:5). The one who 'abides' with Jesus will bear fruit; it happens every time. The one who does not abide in Him does not bear fruit; it cannot happen. Religion without Jesus is fruitless.

The corollary of the connected branch is the severed branch. In the natural world, a branch cut off from the vine is dead, and simply cannot bear fruit. So we, apart from Christ, 'can do nothing.' Each winter at Limerick, when the vines are dormant, we prune the branches, and throw the cuttings into the burn pile. Once a branch is cut off, it remains supple for a short time before it dries and withers, but it has no chance of living on its own. Only the life-giving sap from the vine causes the branch to live, grow, and produce fruit. Thus, Christ's warning: 'If anyone does not abide in me, he is thrown away like a branch and withers; and the branches are gathered, thrown into the fire, and burned' (John 15:6). There is no life in a branch detached from the vine.

Stated differently, all grace is derived from Jesus. It comes only through abiding with Him. 'Abiding' means living together in close communion. As Winthrop described, living with Jesus includes frequent conversations – both the talking part and the listening part – with periods of comfortable silence. Sharing thoughts and daily needs or frustrations. Confessing sin. Sharing meals together. Disclosing hopes and fears, dreams and decisions. He is the wonderful counselor who guides, the mighty God who guards, the everlasting Father who provides, the prince of peace who steadies.

In short, abiding with Christ means having a real, interactive relationship with the living Savior, walking together through life. This is what Peter meant when he challenged believers to 'grow in the grace and knowledge of our Lord and Savior Jesus Christ'

(2 Pet. 3:18). As we walk with Him daily, He strengthens, guides, and changes us. His words change our thinking, our values, and our priorities. We become more like Him, 'growing up in every way into him who is the head, into Christ' (Eph. 4:15).

This spiritual relationship and its transforming influence take place through time spent with the unseen but ever-present Master. Peter knew that communion with the risen Savior would be a spiritual exercise of faith. 'Though you have not seen him, you love him. Though you do not now see him, you believe in him and rejoice with joy that is inexpressible and filled with glory' (1 Pet. 1:8). It is a living relationship that comes from being grafted into Christ, like a branch that is grafted into an olive tree. We draw spiritual life from the branch, and are infused with its life-giving power. 'As the branch cannot bear fruit by itself, unless it abides in the vine, neither can you, unless you abide in me' (John 15:4).

Faith in Christ is a gift. In fact, the root word for grace in Greek is 'charis,' from which we get the English word 'charity.' It is simply a gift, not something we earn. 'For by grace you have been saved through faith. And this is not your own doing, it is the gift of God, not a result of works, so that no one can boast' (Eph. 2:8-9). This may not go over very well with our natural self-esteem, but the reality is that unmerited favor is exactly that – undeserved. We do not and cannot earn it, but only receive it as a free gift.

The giver of a gift chooses the form of the gift, one that fits the needs of the recipient. A parent might bequeath land to one child, while giving others cash or stocks. In love and wisdom, the testator gives according to their differing needs. So it is with faith: the Lord chooses the recipients of the gift and the form of the gift. He has determined that union with the living Christ is the only means of eternal life. Knowing Jesus – the man of grace – is God's inheritance to the nations. At the last day, many will claim to have lived a good life or to have performed great works for God, but Jesus will say to them, 'I never knew you; depart from me, you workers of lawlessness' (Matt. 7:23).

CAN GRACE REALLY TRANSFORM ME?

The ambitious farmer who tills the land and plants a crop is not guaranteed success. He knows he has a fight on his hands, with many forces working against him. The travails of farming are legendary: enduring heat and cold; risking drought and flood; fighting the weeds; fending off pests; patching broken equipment; rushing to harvest; hoping for a market. Farming is a fight all the way! But it is the very struggle that defines and transforms the one who puts his hand to the plow. 'As much as you transform the land by farming, farming transforms you.'[5]

Spiritually, the challenge we all face is how to be transformed from this world into eternal life. God has planted eternity in our hearts, but not the understanding of how to find our way there without His guidance. All of Scripture points to faith in Christ alone to save us.

Ask yourself: do I really trust Christ to bring me safely home, or should I find some other way? The answer is clear: all who follow Christ will be renewed, sustained and transformed by His unfailing grace. You can rest assured the seed of faith will in fact produce a hundredfold at the harvest. 'Grace life' (that is, a life following Jesus) not only saves us, but its authenticity is proven by the way it changes us. No longer conformed to the world, we begin to live transformed lives. The Apostle John put it bluntly: 'By this it is evident who are the children of God … whoever does not practice righteousness is not of God, nor is the one who does not love his brother' (1 John 3:10). God will

---

5. Kristin Kimball, *The Dirty Life: A Memoir of Farming, Food, and Love*, Scribner Books, 2011.

do by His Spirit what we cannot do to change ourselves. As Paul said, 'I am sure of this, that he who began a good work in you will bring it to completion at the day of Christ Jesus' (Phil. 1:6). Each one who is rooted in Christ will be built up. Grace produces fruit, so that God can point to His people in the age to come as examples of the life-giving power of union with Christ.

Ask God for the gift of spiritual wisdom and hunger to grow in your relationship with Christ. Ask for confident hope in the transforming power of His Spirit. God grows rich grace in poor soil, to prove the authority, honor and glory of His Son, both in this world and in the world to come. He causes all things to work together according to His master plan, preparing a magnificent garden in which He and His people will dwell together.

2

THE SOIL

'Those are the ones on whom seed was sown on the good soil; and they hear the word, and accept it, and bear fruit, thirty, sixty, and a hundredfold' (Mark 4:20 NASB).

The so-called Dust Bowl was a period of severe dust storms in America in the 1930s, resulting from a 'perfect storm' of big events. First, a new farming technique arose in the 1920s. The rapid mechanization of gasoline tractors allowed deep plowing of the virgin topsoil of the Great Plains, east of the Rocky Mountains. The formerly grass-covered soil was stripped bare, first burned to remove all grass, then plowed for planting. Millions of acres of the native, short-grass plains of Colorado, New Mexico, Texas, Oklahoma, and Kansas were rapidly converted from native grassland into cultivated crops, such as corn, wheat, and cotton.

Second, the unusually wet decade of the 1920s, which led many to believe the Great Plains region was fertile enough to sustain large-scale farming, was followed by a decade of severe drought in the 1930s. Areas previously averaging ten inches of rainfall annually received almost none, and the newly-exposed topsoil became a sea of dry, powdery, lifeless dust.

Finally, a series of unusual wind storms, especially in 1934, 1936, and 1939, turned the unanchored topsoil into billowing clouds of choking dust, reaching as far as Chicago, New York, and Washington, D.C. John Steinbeck's 1939 Pulitzer Prize winning novel, *The Grapes of Wrath*, captured the misery of the 'Okies,' those displaced, starving residents of Oklahoma who were forced to abandon their farms and homesteads.

As with plant life, so spiritual life begins in the soil of human hearts, where the seed of grace is sown.

SOIL TYPES

Dirt is a complex subject. Scientists have written entire volumes on soil types and soil fertility. Soil types identify the parent material, the age, the density, and the chemistry of the soil. Geologists categorize soil into eleven 'orders,' such as alfisols, ultisols, spodosols, and inceptisols, to name a few, based on the type of material from which it was formed. Differences in mineral content affect plant fertility. Differences in density dictate the ease or difficulty of water movement through the soil. The successful farmer must know the soil before planting a crop, or his efforts may be in vain.

An experienced farmer can often identify a soil's type by its appearance and texture. The color (from white to gray to red to brown to black) and structure (from sand to loam to clay) offer clues to the productivity of the soil. Complicating matters, the depth of the topsoil (the first few inches or feet, where plant roots primarily extend) varies greatly. If plant roots try to extend beyond a thin layer of topsoil but hit an impervious layer of clay or compacted soil (called 'hardpan'), the plants will not thrive.

One expert said, 'The ideal situation is a well-drained topsoil
of at least six inches of loamy material and an underlying loam
to clay subsoil. This provides a deep, well-aerated root zone for
growth, along with a water and nutrient-holding zone to feed
the crop between fertilization and rain events.'[1] Good soil is
essential for a good crop.

HEART TYPES

Just as there are different types of *soils*, Jesus taught that there
are different types of *hearts*. Matthew 13, Mark 4, and Luke 8
(the synoptic gospels) all record His 'parable of the sower.' The
Master Teacher said,

> A sower went out to sow. And as he sowed, some seeds fell
> along the path, and the birds came and devoured them. Other
> seeds fell on rocky ground, where they did not have much
> soil, and immediately they sprang up, since they had no depth
> of soil, but when the sun rose they were scorched. And since
> they had no root, they withered away. Other seeds fell among
> thorns, and the thorns grew up and choked them. Other seeds
> fell on good soil and produced grain, some a hundred-fold,
> some sixty, some thirty (Matt. 13:3-9).

These four distinct areas of the field (the walking path, the rocky
ground beside the path, the thorn-infested ground beyond that,
and, finally, the good soil) illustrate the response of human
hearts to the gospel. The *hard heart* is impervious to the seed,
and it never takes root. 'The evil one comes and snatches away
what has been sown in his heart' (Matt. 13:19). The *shallow
heart* reacts favorably to the gospel, but soon opposition or
difficulty arises, and the plant wilts. 'Immediately he falls

1. Phil Freshley, *Quality Food Plots,* Quality Deer Management
Association, 2006, p. 59.

away' (Matt. 13:21). The *cluttered heart* receives the gospel with joy and the seed begins to grow, but 'the cares of the world and the deceitfulness of riches choke the word, and it proves unfruitful' (Matt. 13:22). Only the *good heart* ultimately yields a crop. 'This is the one who hears the word and understands it. He indeed bears fruit and yields, in one case a hundredfold, in another sixty, and in another thirty' (Matt. 13:23).

Notice that these different hearts share the same time and space, are visited by the same sower, receive the same seed, and enjoy the same amount of rain and sun, but produce very different results. The difference lies in their cultivation. Good soil is soft: it has been plowed and opened, allowing the seeds to take root. Good soil is uncluttered: it is free of rocks, weeds, thorns, and other competitors that hinder or crowd out the young plants. Good soil is deep: it extends beneath the topsoil, so roots can reach deeply into the subsoil for moisture and nutrients. Good soil is nutrient-rich: it contains all the necessary macronutrients and micronutrients to produce healthy plants.

When soil is soft, uncluttered, deep, and rich, the planting conditions are right. So it is with spiritual conditions. And grace is the agent which prepares the heart to receive the seed. The divine farmer does His work, cultivating hearts to receive the word.

God alone can open hearts and 'cause' them to become good soil: Cultivated, Alive, Uncommon, Soft, and Expressive, by His grace.

CULTIVATED

The rudimentary act of scratching the soil to plant seeds has been practiced for millennia. Mattocks and hoes were first used for this tedious, back-breaking, yet essential, task. Without good seed-to-soil contact, germination of the seed and establishment of a viable root system are limited.

Over time, plows and cultivators were invented, to be pulled by draft animals such as oxen, mules or horses. In the 1900s, tractors with internal-combustion engines revolutionized farming. Today, one 40 horsepower tractor can do the work a full team of horses used to accomplish. Greater pulling power also led to the development of specialized equipment for primary tillage (breaking up virgin soil), and various kinds of cultivators or rotary tillers for secondary tillage (final preparation for planting). The harrow (a heavy blade with a curved arm or a series of circular disks, which cut and turn the soil) breaks open the hard ground, and the cultivator (a combination of tines and rollers) stirs and pulverizes the soil to prepare a soft, loose seedbed. Regardless of which method of soil preparation is used, some type of plowing, disking, harrowing, tilling or cultivating is essential. Even the more ecologically friendly twenty-first century practice of 'no-till' farming requires specialized equipment and labor to bury the seed in minimally prepared soil. Whenever you see prepared soil, you know someone has been working. Good soil for cultivated crops does not exist in nature without intervention.

Preparing the soil is the first essential step in growing crops. And none of the subsequent steps takes more effort. It usually requires several passes across a field to prepare the soil adequately. First, the farmer cuts the field in one direction, then re-cuts it crossways to more thoroughly break up the soil. A north-south pass is followed by an east-west pass, and so on, in alternating directions until the soil is soft and powdery. The better prepared the field, the more successful the crop. An ideal seedbed, free of clumps, stones, and debris, only results from diligent preparation.

What is the first step in the Spirit's work of grace? It is the life-giving touch of God, His election, when He places His favor and mercy upon us. We naturally recoil at the idea of predestination or election. Yet, how does dead soil or a fallow field prepare itself? It is helpless without intervention. John Newton wrote,

> Admitting, what I am sure you will admit, the total depravity of human nature, how can we account for the conversion of a soul to God, unless we likewise admit an election of grace? The work must begin somewhere. Either the sinner first seeks the Lord, or the Lord first seeks the sinner. The former is impossible, if by nature we are dead in trespasses and sins.[2]

Seeing how grace is described in the progressive revelation of Scripture is helpful here. There is a Hebrew word used often in the Old Testament that translates into English as 'favor' or 'compassion.' The verb also can be translated 'found grace.' It always describes a person of lower standing who receives an undeserved or unearned blessing from a person of higher standing. In each case, the person of higher authority has compassion on, or bestows favor upon, the lowly, helpless person. Humility evokes compassion; helplessness precedes blessing.

A list of examples may help drive home the point:

- Genesis 6:8 – Noah found favor in the sight of the Lord.
- Genesis 19:19 – Lot found favor in the sight of the angels who rescued him.
- Genesis 32:5 – Jacob found favor in the sight of his older brother, Esau.
- Genesis 39:4 – Joseph found favor in the sight of his master, Potiphar.

---

2. *Select Letters of John Newton*, p. 77.

- Genesis 43:29 – Joseph's brothers found favor in his sight, when Joseph became vice-regent.

- Genesis 47:29 – Jacob on his deathbed found favor in the eyes of his powerful son, Joseph.

- Genesis 50:4 – Joseph found favor in the eyes of Pharaoh.

- Ruth 2:10 – Ruth found favor in the eyes of her wealthy kinsman-redeemer, Boaz.

- 1 Sam. 1:18 – Hannah found favor in the eyes of the chief priest, Eli.

- Esther 2:17 – Esther found favor in the eyes of King Ahasuerus.

- Daniel 1:9 – Daniel found favor in the eyes of the chief eunuch.

Each time, a recognition of helplessness and a cry for help drew a compassionate response (grace) from the person of higher authority. True humility is waking up to the realization that I can do nothing for myself. That is the spark of life, a heart prepared to receive grace. The regenerating work of the Spirit has quickened my lifeless soul, opening my eyes to my own helplessness.

This is what Jesus meant when He said we must be *born again*. 'Unless one is born again, he cannot see the kingdom of God' (John 3:3). Without the life-giving, awakening touch of the Spirit, we are powerless to save ourselves. Humility is a sure sign that the Spirit has already been at work.

'Receive with meekness the implanted word, which is able to save your souls' (James 1:21). The Lord's tool for breaking and humbling us may come through life's troubles, pains, disappointments, or disillusionments, using them to break open our naturally hard hearts. By grace, they cause us to cry out for mercy. And a sincere cry for mercy always finds favor in the eyes of the Lord.

On March 9, 1748, John Newton, a profane, proud and angry young slave-trader, went to sleep aboard his ship, the *Greyhound*, a hardened, impenitent man. 'I went to bed that night in my usual security and indifference, but was awakened from a sound sleep by the force of a violent sea that broke on us ... This alarm was followed by a cry from the deck that the ship was going down or sinking.' In the harrowing hours until daybreak on March 10, some of the crew, all of the livestock, and most of the cargo were lost, swept overboard. Exhausted and fearful, Newton was overtaken by a deep sense of dread, and he said aloud to the captain, 'The Lord have mercy on us.' Both men were astonished at his statement. 'I was instantly struck by my own words. This was the first desire I had breathed for mercy for many years.'[3]

Grace first softens hard hearts.

ALIVE

One of the mottos of the Protestant Reformation in the 1500s and 1600s was 'sola gratia,' or 'by grace alone.' Scripture teaches us that from the time of our physical birth we are spiritually dead, because the DNA of original sin is carried by the entire human race. 'But God, being rich in mercy, because of the great love with which he loved us, even when we were dead in our trespasses, made us alive together with Christ – by grace you have been saved' (Eph. 2:4-5). Grace takes what is dead, and makes it alive. God does so by breathing new life into us. 'I will give you a new heart, and a new spirit I will put within you. And I will remove the heart of stone from your flesh and

---

3. John Newton quoted in Jonathan Aitken, *John Newton: From Disgrace to Amazing Grace*, Crossway, 2007, p. 76.

give you a new heart of flesh. And I will put my Spirit within you ... and you shall be my people, and I will be your God' (Ezek. 36: 26-28).

Soil may seem dead to the unobservant eye, but beneath the surface is an entire ecosystem teaming with life. Vast root systems from all kinds of plants, shrubs and trees that draw moisture from the soil. Microorganisms, including millions of bacteria, bugs, insects, earthworms, mice, moles, gophers and other ground-dwellers, that burrow and turn the soil. Add 'bioturbation,' the shifting of soil created by wind, water, earthquakes, volcanos, wildfires, and human disturbance, and the soil is a lively and ever-changing environment.

In the prior chapter, we met John and Molly Chester, in their years-long battle to establish an organic apricot farm in a wasteland. The wonderful documentary, 'The Biggest Little Farm,' follows their epic struggle against pests, predators, and wildfires.

The Chesters' first job, however, was to pump life back into the hard, dry, compacted, and lifeless topsoil at the industrial site they purchased. So, they took tons of livestock manure, mixed in thousands of gallons of water, cooked the mixture in a large cauldron to jumpstart the growth of microorganisms, and irrigated their fields with this rich 'poo brew.' Voilà! Soon the ground was alive with all kinds of nutrients and microscopic critters.

Scientists say plants need thirteen essential elements for growth. They subdivide these elements into two categories: six 'macronutrients,' which plants need in large amounts, and seven 'micronutrients,' only needed in small quantities. The macronutrients are nitrogen, phosphorus, potassium, calcium, magnesium and sulfur. The micronutrients include iron, manganese, copper, zinc, boron, molybdenum (don't even try to pronounce it), and chlorine.

When you visit a garden center to buy fertilizer, the three numbers typically displayed on the bag list the quantities of the first three macronutrients. For example, garden variety '10-10-10' fertilizer contains 10% nitrogen, 10% phosphorus, and 10% potassium by weight. Therefore, a fifty-pound bag of 10-10-10 contains five pounds of nitrogen, five pounds of phosphorus, five pounds of potassium, plus thirty-five pounds of other macro- and micro-nutrients and inert matter. Optimum plant growth requires the proper amount of all thirteen elements.

But there is more. The way plants physically absorb these nutrients at the molecular level is also complex. The key factor is the amount of hydrogen in the soil, which enables the plant's cells to attach, move, and assimilate available nutrients. This is known as soil acidity or 'pH' for the 'power of Hydrogen.' Alkaline or basic soil is hydrogen-rich, while acidic soil is hydrogen-deprived. Hydrogen is the transfer agent that picks up the essential nutrients and carries them though the cellular membrane. In the same way, the Holy Spirit is the agent that transports grace into the human soul.

Because of the varying density, mineral content, and acidity of different soil types, the amount of work it takes to prepare the soil and the quantity of lime and fertilizer needed to amend the soil also varies. Some soil is just easier to work with than others. So it is with people.

Like soil nutrients, there are certain characteristics that could be called the macronutrients of grace. These are the elements necessary to produce spiritual growth. Such attributes only exist in a soul that is humble before God and, therefore, humble in relationships with others. The pH must be right: 'personal Humility!' Scripture says, 'To the humble he gives favor' (Prov. 3:34).

Jesus listed the essential elements of good soil in His well-known Sermon on the Mount. These elements of grace include poverty of spirit, mourning, meekness, hungering and thirsting for righteousness, mercy, purity in heart, peacemaking, and willingness to suffer for the sake of righteousness (Matt. 5:3-10).

We can think of these eight characteristics as the macronutrients of grace, found only in the soul that has been amended by the Spirit. The soul without these elements cannot produce spiritual fruit.

To be *poor in spirit* has nothing to do with one's financial condition. The 'poor man' in Scripture is the person who realizes his spiritual bankruptcy, and looks to God for all his spiritual needs. 'This poor man cried, and the LORD heard him and saved him out of all his troubles' (Ps. 34:6). Poverty of spirit leads to acknowledgement of sin, and the result is eternal life: 'theirs is the kingdom of heaven.'

The person who *mourns* recognizes his sinfulness, regrets the mess he has made of his life, and desperately wants to change his wretched ways. He knows he stinks. Spiritual mourning leads to deep contrition for sin, and the result is forgiveness: 'they shall be comforted.'

The *meek* person does not insist on his own way, assert his own opinions, or demand that God and others accommodate themselves to his wishes. Meekness leads to humility and gentleness in dealing with others, and the result is astounding: 'they shall inherit the earth.'

The one who *hungers and thirsts for righteousness* has a deep longing to grow in grace, and therefore pursues a relationship with the Lord diligently. Hungering and thirsting leads to teach-ability, and the result is the restoration of right relationships: 'they shall be satisfied.'

The person who is *merciful* knows that he found favor when he did not deserve it, and therefore he has a charitable attitude toward others who do not deserve it. Mercy leads to a recognition of the pain and distress of others, and the result is compassion reciprocated: 'they shall find mercy.'

The *pure in heart* are consistent on the inside and on the outside, not operating with hidden motives. Heart purity leads to sincerity and transparency in our words and actions, and the result is standing before the Lord: 'they shall see God.'

The *peacemakers* are the ones who have been reconciled with God and, therefore, strive to live at peace with others. Peacemakers work at building peace, and the result is an increasing family likeness: 'they shall be called sons of God.'

Those who are *persecuted for righteousness' sake* entrust themselves fully to their loving Father, even when the world is at war with them. The Spirit adds a unique quality to such individuals, in that they rejoice to be honored to suffer for Christ's sake. And the result again transcends this life: 'theirs is the kingdom of heaven.'

Eight times, Jesus said anyone with these essential attributes is 'blessed.' To say that the person with these characteristics is blessed could likewise be translated that they are 'fertile.' He or she will bear fruit, for the essential elements of grace are present in the soil. The Spirit of grace quickens the heart and breathes life into dead souls.

UNCOMMON

Good dirt is hard to find. In fact, land brokers, farmers and ranchers often study United States Department of Agriculture (USDA) and Natural Resources Conservation Service (NRCS) soil maps to locate property with good soil. Soil quality can vary from one portion of a tract to another, within the span of a few acres. The rare soil with adequate moisture, available nutrients, and manageable structure is highly sought after for maximizing yields.

In the parable of the sower, as we have seen, Jesus described four kinds of human soil: those with hard hearts, shallow hearts, cluttered hearts, and good hearts. Notice that, in some sense, those who will bear fruit are a minority. In the words of Christ, the seed will be 'snatched away' from the hard soil. The seed will 'fade away' in the rocky soil. The seed will be 'choked out and prove unfruitful' in the cluttered soil. Only the good soil will 'accept it and bear fruit.' Four types of soil, yet only one that is productive. Jesus never pulled any punches: not every person has grace.

Did Jesus mean that precisely one-fourth of humanity will be saved? Probably not. The Book of Revelation says that heaven will be populated with countless multitudes of God's people from every tongue, tribe and nation on earth. Yet not all will be saved. In relative terms, the majority will perish and the minority, a remnant, will be saved. A heart hardened to the gospel rejects it. A heart open to the gospel runs to Christ and loves His word. Grace abounds for everyone who looks to Jesus.

This is why Jesus said, 'The gate is wide and the way is easy that leads to destruction, and those who enter by it are many. The gate is narrow and the way is hard that leads to eternal life, and those who find it are few' (Matt. 7:13-14). The wide gate represents the many ways that people may try to enter eternal life, through their own good works and the many false religions. But the gate is narrow that leads to eternal life, because it is one specific door. Jesus said He alone is the door by which the sheep must enter the sheepfold. And the way is hard, meaning that only as we are cultivated – turned from our sinful nature into a newness of life – will we persevere and bear fruit. Life may beat us up and break us down, but if, by grace, we turn to Christ, the hard way is the best way. Christ alone is the way, the truth, and the life.

The good news of the gospel is that, though we are all sinners, God provided a substitute to pay the penalty for our sin. Only a relationship with this Savior, our Redeemer, reconciles us with God. We find peace with God through the sacrifice of our Lord Jesus Christ, and through Him we live in the kingdom of grace. Our old self has been crucified in Christ, and the life we now live in the flesh, we live by faith in the Son of God, who loved us and gave Himself for us (Gal. 2:20).

SOFT

A plowed field is a pleasure to tread. The ground is not only free of weeds and clutter, but its most striking feature is its softness. Boots sink into the surface with every step. The soil is loose, and ready to receive the seed. So it is in the spiritual realm. Peter called this 'a tender heart, a humble mind' (1 Pet. 3:8).

Jesus also described what happens when the gospel seed is sown on soft ground. Matthew's record of the parable of the sower says the good soil is that which receives the word and 'understands it.' Mark's version says the good soil 'accepts it.' Luke's recounting says the good soil 'holds it fast.' Apparently, Jesus taught this parable on many occasions to His disciples, using slight variations in wording. But all three essentially mean the same thing: the good soil recognizes, receives, and retains the truth of the gospel. The seed is snatched away from hard soil by predators, wilts from the sun in shallow soil, or is choked by the cares of the world in cluttered soil. Only the good soil receives and retains the abiding word.

A good heart is a soft heart is a humble heart. And without the life-giving intervention of the Lord, the soil of our heart remains hard and dead.

EXPRESSIVE

Wildlife managers often say that a whitetail deer with massive antlers has 'expressed his full potential.' By a combination of age and access to high-quality forage, a mature buck's rack reaches the greatest size he is genetically capable of producing. He is in full glory.

When planting crops for the wildlife at Limerick, I often buy seed from Luther Wannamaker at L.B. Wannamaker Seed Company in St. Matthews, South Carolina. One of his most popular seed blends for warm-season crops (and anyone who's been to South Carolina in the summer knows it is 'warm') is a mixture he calls 'Magic Carpet.' In a stroke of marketing genius, the name alone conjures up visions of a rich, green carpet of forage. A 50-pound bag of Magic Carpet contains 43% soybeans (21.5 pounds), 43% iron and clay peas (21.5 pounds), 6% sunflowers (3 pounds), 4% buckwheat (2 pounds), 2% brown-top millet (1 pound), and 2% 'other crops, weeds, and inert matter.' Yet this 50-pound bag of mixed seeds can produce literally tons of leafy forage for the wildlife to consume. In moderately good soil, it yields about 1,500 pounds of edible stems and leaves (thirty-fold). In better soil, perhaps 3,000 pounds (sixty-fold). And in really good soil, up to 5,000 pounds (a hundred-fold). Good soil expresses the full potential of the seed.

So, there we have it: rich soil is cultivated, alive, uncommon, soft, and expressive. Trouble is, I know my heart, and it is made of very poor soil. It is desperately wicked, hard and dry. Like Apricot Lane Farms, I need a steady infusion of living water, full of fresh nutrients, to bring my dead heart to life. Jesus gives us that living water, refreshing the soul and preparing it to produce a great harvest. Grace prepares the soil!

3

THE SEED

'You have been born again, not of perishable seed but of imperishable, through the living and abiding word of God'
(1 Pet.1:23).

When it comes to our health, what we are NOT doing is killing us. And I'm not even talking about exercise. The 'Global Burden of Disease Study,' a long-term study of a large cohort of people around the world, determined that simply not eating enough nuts and seeds is a major dietary risk factor for death and disability.

Eating a handful (about a quarter cup) of walnuts, almonds, pistachios, pecans, sunflower or other seeds five or more days a week will increase life span on average by two years.[1]

Why are seeds and nuts so healthful? Because they are seeds! They contain the whole complex of nutrients and energy to produce a new plant or seedling, all in one, tasty little package.

---

1. Dr. Michael Greger, *How Not To Die*, Flatiron Books, 2015, p. 342.

The physical world mirrors the spiritual realm, where life begins with a seed. Acorns produce oak trees. Pine seeds produce pine trees. Each seed is a small, self-contained package that holds the genetic code of life. The power of life is in the seed. As the germination of a seed is a miracle, the spark of spiritual life in a human soul is a miracle of God's grace. It's by grace alone, as God plants the seed of faith in our hearts and causes it to germinate.

The seed God plants in us is His Word. 'The sower sows the word' (Mark 4:14). What word? Though the Bible uses various terms to describe God's written revelation ('scripture,' 'sacred writings,' 'implanted word,' and 'sound words,' to name a few), the most common is simply His 'word.' As in, 'Your word is a light to my feet and a lamp to my path' (Psalm 119:105). Or, 'This word is the good news that was preached to you' (1 Pet. 1:25).

Scripture says the seed of the word is abiding, living, imperishable, valuable, and effectual. In other words, it is ALIVE.

ABIDING

Look in the dictionary, and the word 'abide' simply means to remain, to continue, to stay. Seeds abiding in a cool, dry place may remain dormant for many years. But plant the seeds in the ground during growing season, allow them to remain (to abide) in the warm, moist soil, and they begin to sprout. The seed must remain, continue, stay in the soil in order to germinate, put down roots, and grow.

So it is with God's Word. No abiding, no germination. The Apostle Paul taught this basic principle of the seed: 'let the word of Christ dwell in you richly' (Col. 3:16). As the words of

Christ abide in our hearts and minds, they begin to germinate and take root.

My friend, William MacKenzie, is a sheep and arable farmer near Inverness in the north of Scotland. But above all, he is a follower of Christ who loves God's word. When William and his brothers were growing up, their father led the family in devotions and the singing of a psalm from the Scottish Psalter every morning and every evening. By the time William left home, he had sung through the psalms thousands of times. To this day, he can recite many of the psalms by heart, and his conversation is sprinkled with Bible quotations. If a person is down, William has a verse to cheer them. If fearful, he has a psalm to comfort them. If happy, he has a word to rejoice with them. That is what it means for God's word to dwell in us richly.

The challenge of letting the word abide in us richly is how to get it into our minds and retain it. Our schedules are full, and most of us cannot memorize things easily. So, how are we to do it?

Two key habits for every believer are memorization and meditation. The first step is to take a verse or passage, write it out by hand, and read it aloud over and over. Try drawing a map or diagram of the passage, using colored pens or pencils, different fonts and sizes for key words, various shapes, and graphic images. For example, if you wanted to memorize the answer to question and answer four of the Westminster Shorter Catechism (Q: 'What is God?' A: 'God is a Spirit, infinite, eternal, and unchangeable, in his being, wisdom, power, holiness, justice, goodness, and truth') you might imagine the sunrise, with radiant beams, like this:

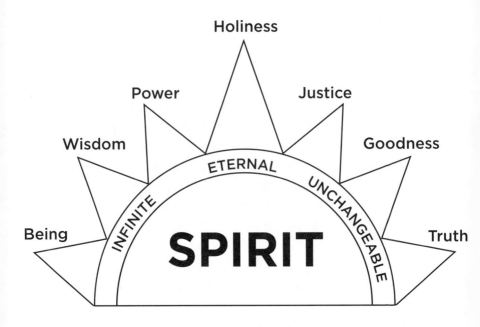

By engaging the hands, both the right (artistic) and left (logical) sides of our brain, and even our voice to repeat aloud, we better internalize the pattern and flow of the words. Repeat the text over and over, checking frequently to see if any words were left out. Try to create mental 'hooks,' such as acronyms or mental images, to help the words stick more readily in your mind. Memorization and meditation are sweet little M&M's for the soul.

When my ninety-year-old mother-in-law, Ann Edwards, was about to go into major surgery, we sat together in a small hospital room. 'I need a word to calm me,' she said. We recited together my wife's favorite verse, Isaiah 41:10, over and over. 'Fear not, for I am with you; be not dismayed, for I am your God; I will strengthen you, I will help you, I will uphold you with my righteous right hand.' To ingrain the words, we repeated the acrostic 'SHU,' as in 'shoo away' the fear. Strengthen, help, uphold. Strengthen, help, uphold. When Ann awoke from the anesthesia several hours later, she looked up and said, 'I will strengthen you, I will help you, I will uphold you with my righteous right hand.'

The practice of 'meditation' may have a negative connotation for many, because of its association with Eastern religions. But meditating on Scripture is foundational for the Christian. The goal is not emptying our minds, but rather filling our minds. Select a passage of Scripture, and repeat the words over and over, perhaps while driving, exercising, or sitting quietly with a cup of coffee. What does the text teach me? How does it apply to my life right now? How can I convert these words into a prayer for myself and others?

Years ago, I remember studying the parables of Jesus on Saturday mornings in preparation for a series of Bible lessons, then going to the farm and spending hours on the tractor, plowing the fields. As I bounced along to the roar of a diesel engine, I turned the stories over and over in my mind. Like the soil being stirred, fresh insights and new convictions began to emerge. In the same way, a long walk, a quiet drive, a restful chair in the morning or evening, after reading Scripture, often yields rich prayer times and reflection.

Abraham Kuyper, prime minister of the Netherlands and seminary professor in the early 1900s, adopted the habit of taking long walks every afternoon to meditate, pray, and think about things he needed to do. The spiritual (and physical!) benefits were impressive. Jonathan Edwards, the great American theologian in the 1700s, often took long, casual horseback rides through the New England countryside. 'Once, as I rode out into the woods … having alighted from my horse in a retired place, as my manner commonly has been, to walk for divine contemplation and prayer, I had a view that for me was extraordinary, of the glory of the Son of God, as Mediator between God and man, and his wonderful, great, full, pure, and sweet grace and love, and meek and gentle condescension.'[2]

The habit of Bible intake plus spiritual rumination is like a cow grazing in a pasture, then lying down in the shade to chew its cud. As we take time to roll the text over and over in our thoughts, the Holy Spirit gives fresh insights, reveals our sin, and brings practical applications to mind. Thus, He assimilates the word into our souls, in the same way our body absorbs nutrients from food. Read, write, recite, reflect. Grace incorporates Biblical truth into our souls, as the Word abides in us.

LIVING

Peter says the word of God is also 'living.' Just like a natural seed, such as a kernel of corn or a grain of wheat, may seem dormant, yet plant it and watch it grow. There is life in that package! So it is with Scripture. Plant it, and something amazing happens. 'For the word of God is living and active, sharper than any two-edged sword, piercing to the division of soul and of spirit, of joints and of marrow, and discerning the thoughts and intentions of the heart' (Heb. 4:12). Scripture is the living-change agent that performs its work in us, revealing our thoughts and motives, reproving us, correcting us, and making us change direction.

The Bible is not just another book. It is fundamentally and organically different from all other human writings. It is the tool of God to redeem the world: 'So shall my word be that goes out from my mouth; it shall not return empty, but it shall accomplish that which I purpose, and shall succeed in the thing for which I sent it' (Isa. 55:11). 'All Scripture is breathed out by

---

2. Quoted in Iain Murray, *Jonathan Edwards: A New Biography,* The Banner of Truth Trust, 1987, p. 100.

God' (2 Tim. 3:16). It is the inspired word of God, written by men 'as they were carried along by the Holy Spirit' (2 Pet. 1:21). As Paul said to the believers in Thessalonica, 'You accepted it not as the word of men, but as what it really is, the word of God, which is at work in you believers' (1 Thess. 2:13).

Jesus made it clear to His disciples that the seed of His Word holds the code of eternal life. 'The words that I have spoken to you are spirit and life' (John 6:63). The kingdom principle is profound: Scripture is dynamic, like living yeast which spreads throughout a lump of dough, changing its chemistry. As we hide God's Word in our heart, it changes our thoughts, desires, habits, and perspectives.

IMPERISHABLE

The word 'imperishable' means non-fading, non-destructible, never going to perish. In other words, God's immutable truth will last forever. The Apostle John emphasized this when he described Jesus in the prologue to his Gospel. 'In the beginning was the Word, and the Word was with God, and the Word was God. He was in the beginning with God' (John 1:1-2). Jesus had no beginning and will have no end. His words likewise remain established and will have no end. The most stable elements in the world, such as silver and gold, will perish, but God's Word is imperishable. Peter puts it this way, quoting a passage from the prophet Isaiah: 'The grass withers, and the flower falls, but the word of the Lord remains forever' (1 Pet. 1:24-25).

This means, among other things, that God's Word applies to all people, in all cultures, at all times in history. It never fades in relevance or potency, no matter the circumstances of our lives or the times in which we live. It also means that it is the most stable thing in my world. The people we love may die; the circumstances of our life or health may change radically, but the Word remains the solid foundation on which we stand. Treasure it as the imperishable seed that it is – value it above all other things, and make Bible intake a priority over perishable, worldly things.

VALUABLE

We have two words in English that mean a similar thing, but in differing degrees. 'Valuable' means costly or precious. 'Invaluable' means so costly or precious that it is beyond valuation. God's Word falls into the second category. It is 'more to be desired than gold, even much fine gold; sweeter also than honey and drippings from the honeycomb' (Ps. 19:10).

In professional bicycle races, such as the Tour de France, the mountain climbs are rated by degree of difficulty for their length, elevation gain, and location within the race (near the beginning, while the riders are fresh, or near the end, when the riders are exhausted). Four categories from one (most difficult) to four (least difficult) rank the degree of difficulty, but a few of the most monstrously difficult climbs are considered 'uncategorized' (*hors catégorie*). In a positive way, God's words claim to be beyond categorization in eternal weight and value. How valuable is God's Word to you?

My friend, Dr. Alexandre Ponomarov, was born in St. Petersburg, Russia, in 1949. Growing up in the communist environment of the U.S.S.R., owning a Bible was strictly forbidden by law, and atheism was the state religion. Yet the Holy Spirit began to stir in his heart when Alex was a young nuclear physicist within the Soviet defense department; he was hungry to read God's Word. His wife, Irina, also a PhD., saved a year of her salary to buy Alex a fragment of a black-market Bible, which included the Gospel of John. Reading the words of Jesus changed his life radically, and he ultimately fled the U.S.S.R and sought asylum in the United States to pursue a seminary degree at Reformed Theological Seminary in Jackson, Mississippi. Like the disciples who left their fishing nets to follow Jesus, Alex and Irina walked away from careers and nearly everything valuable in their lives, for the sake of the Word.

When I plant or sow seed at the farm, I have a strong, instinctive reaction if I accidentally spill seed on the ground while loading the planter or the spreader. I anxiously try to pick up every last seed, though there were millions of them in the bag, lest they go to waste. For God, every word is precious, and not one word will fall away or be wasted. Every word of Scripture is valuable, and is profitable for teaching, instructing, correcting, and training His people.

EFFECTUAL

A corollary to the living, imperishable nature of the seed, in and of itself, is its power to change the human soul in which it abides. When Jesus prayed for His disciples and for all in future generations who would believe through them, He asked His Father to 'Sanctify them in the truth; your word is truth' (John 17:17). When Paul wrote to the Thessalonian believers, he said he thanked God that 'when you received the word of God … you accepted it not as the word of man but as what it really is, the word of God, *which is at work in you believers*' (1 Thess. 2:13, my emphasis). The word does not remain dormant, but germinates, takes root, and starts to grow in the heart of the believer. The growing seed effects deep changes in our thought patterns, secret motives, core values, personal interests, and typical behavior.

The kingdom of grace is always growing and expanding, and God's lovely word is the tool He uses to change us. 'So shall my word be that goes out from my mouth; it shall not return to me empty, but it shall accomplish that which I purpose, and shall succeed in the thing for which I sent it' (Isa. 55:11). Despite the relativism of our age, there is objective, moral truth which was established by God when He created the universe, and all who accept the truth of the gospel will be changed by it. All who oppose the truth of the gospel will be broken down by it.

The term 'effectual grace' has been used for centuries to describe the power of God's word, applied by the regenerating work of the Holy Spirit, to bring real transformation to the soul. The Westminster Confession of Faith, written in 1646, described this effectual calling: 'by his word and Spirit, out of that state of sin and death in which they are by nature, to grace and salvation by Jesus Christ, enlightening their minds spiritually and savingly to understand the things of God; taking away their heart of stone and giving them a heart of flesh.'[3] The word of God is effective to bring all who are called into a saving relationship with Jesus.

Because God's word is Abiding, Living, Imperishable, Valuable, and Effectual, the grace which inspired it will see that it grows and bears fruit.

GRACE PROTECTS THE SEED

After seeds are first sown or planted, they are particularly fragile and vulnerable. A light covering of soil provides a warm, moist environment for germination. But it also protects the seeds from predators. Birds, squirrels, raccoons, deer, turkeys, and hogs quickly flock to the fields to eat the seeds.

One day, I sowed a mixture of wheat and oats in a winter food plot, then drove the tractor to the equipment shed to drop off the spreader and pick up a 'cultipacker' to press the seeds into the soft ground. In the thirty minutes it took to swap

---

3. Westminster Confession of Faith, Chapter X.

implements and return to the field, a flock of wild turkeys had already descended on the scene, and were devouring the exposed seeds.

Turkeys are one thing; raccoons are another. The smarter the enemy, the more destructive his ways. It is maddening to watch a family of raccoons methodically dig up the furrows of a freshly planted corn or soybean field, feasting on the seeds. Farmers use many kinds of deterrents, from scarecrows to electric fences, from chemical sprays to bullets, to protect the vulnerable seeds until they take root!

The enemy of our souls is like those predators, only smarter. Jesus warned in the parable of the sower and the seeds that 'some seed fell along the path, and the birds came and devoured it' (Mark 4:4). He later explained to His disciples, 'These are the ones along the path, where the word is sown: when they hear, Satan immediately comes and takes away the word that is sown in them' (Mark 4:15). If the Lord does not protect the seed from scavengers, it will be snatched away and devoured.

The person who abides in Christ need not fear the scavengers. No matter how fragile faith may seem, His promise is that we live under the divine protection of the Almighty. 'In the shadow of your wings I will take refuge, till the storms of destruction pass by' (Ps. 57:1). When Peter wrote to believers scattered by persecution, he warned them that Satan prowls around, seeking someone to devour. But 'the God of all grace, who has called you to his eternal glory in Christ, will himself restore, confirm, strengthen, and establish you' (1 Pet. 5:10).

GRACE GERMINATES

Seeds are dormant, existing in a suspended state of lifelessness, which we are powerless to unlock. Farmers may create the right conditions, closely monitoring soil temperature, moisture, and nutrients, but God alone provides the spark of life. Man's inability to understand, much less to replicate, the spark of natural life is astounding. 'The seed sprouts and grows; he knows not how' (Mark 4:27).

The power of spiritual life also belongs exclusively to God. John Newton said,

> By nature we are all dead in trespasses and sins, not only strangers to God, but in a state of enmity and opposition to his government and grace. In this respect, whatever difference there may be in characters of men as members of society, they are all, whether wise or ignorant, whether sober or profane, equally incapable of receiving or approving divine truths, I Corinthians 2:14. On this ground, the Lord declares, 'No man can come unto me, except the Father who has sent me draws him.'[4]

Seeds have a moment of germination, when they change from death to life. Seeds can be stored in a cool, dry place such as barn or storehouse for years, even decades, then when planted spring to life. The believer's moment of germination is when he comes in contact with the Savior, and his soul awakens. 'As you do not know the way the spirit comes to the bones in the womb of a woman with child, so you do not know the work of God who makes everything' (Eccles. 11:5). This divine spark of life is unmistakable: 'When the Gentiles heard [the Gospel], they began rejoicing and glorifying the word of the Lord, and as many as were appointed to eternal life believed' (Acts 13:48).

The moment of germination is when Jesus introduces Himself into someone's life. Jesus called this being 'born again' (John 3:3). This relationship with the Lord, by His Spirit, is hard to define, but impossible to mistake. Grace is not found in being religious. Grace is not a reward earned for doing good

---

4. *Select Letters of John Newton*, p. 1.

things. Grace is found in knowing Jesus. And once He comes into our life, He *becomes* our life.

A fundamental truth of the gospel is that the believer is alive because he or she is joined to Christ. Often referred to as 'communion' or 'union' with Christ, we can think of spiritual birth as sharing in Christ's life. Purchased grace goes so far as to say that the things Christ did, we have done with Him. We are said to have been baptized with Christ (Rom. 6:3), crucified with Christ (Gal. 2:20), died with Christ (2 Tim. 2:11), raised with Christ (Eph. 2:6), made alive with Christ (Eph. 2:5), and, therefore, are joint heirs with Christ (Rom. 8:17). In other words, our lives are hidden (planted) in Christ. 'If any man is in Christ, he is a new creation' (2 Cor. 5:17).

Even more poignantly, not only are we 'in Christ' by faith, but Christ is also in us! This is the death-defying, dormancy-ending power of grace. 'It is no longer I who lives, but Christ who lives in me' (Gal. 2:20). Therefore, we are no longer slaves to sin: 'Do you not realize this about yourselves, that Jesus Christ is in you?' (2 Cor. 13:5). This also explains why we will, and indeed must, live forever with Him in glory: 'To them God chose to make known how great among the Gentiles are the riches of the glory of this mystery, which is Christ in you, the hope of glory' (Col. 1:27).

All of these benefits of grace are gifts from Christ, not on the basis of merit, that no one should boast. As we said earlier, John Owen called the believer's standing before God 'purchased grace,' which Christ procured for us by His obedience, His suffering and death, His resurrection, and His continual intercession for us before the throne of God. 'Purchased grace is the grace of privilege.'[5]

---

5. John Owen, *Communion With God*, The Banner of Truth Trust, 2013, p. 118.

In 1977, while I was a student at Clemson University, the governor of Florida called and invited a small group of to us to attend the Gator Bowl. 'Please come to Jacksonville as my guests, to see Clemson play the University of Pittsburgh.' He sent a private jet to Columbia, put us up in luxury accommodations, and assigned a Florida state trooper to transport us from place to place, including entrance into the governor's private box on game day. It was a glorious and heady experience. Oh, did I mention that the governor's invitation was issued to my future father-in-law, Jim Edwards, who was then serving as governor of South Carolina? I was just along as a guest of the honoree. So it is with our privileges in Christ. We are strictly included in the inner circle because we are His adopted family.

The Apostle Paul described his own salvation or spiritual germination in these terms: 'He who had set me apart before I was born, and who called me by his grace, was pleased to reveal his Son to me' (Gal. 1:15-16). John Newton, the eighteenth-century slave trader who came to faith in Christ and later became a pastor, described the spark of spiritual life this way:

> The beginning of this work is instantaneous. It is effected by a certain kind of light communicated to the soul, to which it was before an utter stranger. The eyes of the understanding are opened and enlightened. The light at first afforded is weak and indistinct, like the morning dawn; but when it is once begun, it will certainly increase and spread to the perfect day.[6]

This spark of life is a gift, not something we figure out with our minds or earn by our merits. 'But God, being rich in mercy, because of the great love with which he loved us, even when we were dead in our trespasses, made us alive together with Christ – by grace you have been saved – and raised us up with him' (Eph. 2: 4-6). The fact that salvation is a gift, not something

---

6. *Select Letters of John Newton*, p. 2.

we earn, gives us ultimate comfort. If we had to earn our way to heaven, how much would be enough? Does my 'badness' outweigh my 'goodness' on the scales of God's justice? How would I ever know that I have found favor with God? But the beauty of grace is that the outcome is sure. Be comforted! It is not our works that save us, but Christ's work alone. It is not our victory over sin and death that matters, but Christ's alone. Jesus is the source of our life, and from His fullness, we have all received grace upon grace.

SOW IT THICK!

One day, I sought planting advice from Rusty Williams, the owner of a small feed and seed store in Moncks Corner, South Carolina. While telling me how much seed to use per acre for a certain kind of oats, Rusty made a profound statement: 'You can't sow it too thick. If it's thick enough, the oats will crowd out the weeds, and make a great crop.'

If the word of God is like seed, then 'sow it thick' is great advice for us as believers, at every stage of our spiritual walk. The more we read, mark, learn, and inwardly digest Scripture, the more we grow in grace.

A friend once told me that her ninety-three-year-old father, a marginal church-goer all his life, had recently changed churches and joined a Bible study. He was spending hours daily working on Bible lessons, and a major transformation was taking place in his personality and priorities in life. She said, 'I've been shocked. It's like someone took an old stump, fertilized it, and it sprouted new growth. He's so excited about his relationship with the Lord, I keep asking myself, "Is this really the same man I've known all my life?"'

Advertising agencies know that the secret of marketing lies in repetition, repetition, repetition. The same message, the same logo, the same refrain used over and over creates brand awareness, and leads to brand loyalty. They attach a catchy phrase or a snappy jingle to make the message stick with us. So it is with the seed of God's word. Sow it thick, and ingest it constantly.

The life-changing power of grace is in the seed! And the seed is the Word of God.

THE SEED IS JESUS

The life of grace, at its most basic, is about a relationship with Jesus. Listening to His voice, as He speaks to us through His Word; talking with Him in prayer; communing with Him as we go through each day. This relationship is what transforms us from the inside out. He who has the Son has the life; he who does not have the Son of God does not have the life.

The grace of life is in the seed of His Word.

4

THE GROWTH

'The word of truth ... is bearing fruit and growing – as it also does among you, since the day you heard it and understood the grace of God in truth' (Col. 1:5-6).

The American alligator (*Alligator mississippiensis*) inhabits ponds and freshwater swamps throughout the Southeastern U.S., from Texas through North Carolina. A skilled predator, it feeds primarily on fish, turtles, snakes, and small mammals, though occasionally on larger prey, including humans. An American alligator can live 50 to 70 years, with mature males weighing over 1,000 pounds.

But life starts small for young alligators. A gator hatchling is only six to eight inches long, with an early growth phase for males of eight to ten inches per year, until it reaches 10 to 14 feet on average. Thereafter, it adds only a few inches per year, until it stops growing. The record male gator from Louisiana was reportedly over 19 feet long.

What is the spiritual growth pattern for a believer? The pattern generally follows, not that of an alligator, but that of a seed.

GRACE TAKES ROOT

Once germination occurs, seeds begin to put down roots. The first stage of growth is not upwards, but downwards. Seeds can sprout almost anywhere, even in a shallow crevice of a driveway or a rock, but if they never establish a root system, they quickly die. Pastor John Newton put it this way:

> Though the seed may seem to spring up, and look green for a season, if there be not depth for it to take root, it will surely wither away. We may be unable to judge with certainty upon the first appearance of a religious profession, whether the work be thus deep and spiritual or not; but 'the Lord knows them that are his'; and wherever it is real, it is an infallible token of salvation.[1]

The principle of irrepressible growth is imbedded in every believer. Once true grace sprouts, growth happens.

But how do we know if grace has taken root? The answer is first found in the believer's relationship to the living Lord Jesus. It is only by a true, personal connection with Jesus that the seed of life is established. Paul was so radically changed after meeting Jesus that he described himself this way, 'It is no longer I who live, but Christ who lives in me. And the life I now live in the flesh, I live by faith in the Son of God, who loved me and gave himself for me' (Gal. 2:20). Grace is Christ living in us, producing the fundamental changes that lead to our growth and His glory.

---

1. *Select Letters of John Newton*, p. 3.

One good indicator that a person is connected to Christ is their hunger for His words. The love of Scripture is a sign of grace at work, an evidence of spiritual life. As we saw earlier in the parable of the sower and the seed, Jesus provided a clue about the source of all spiritual growth. Matthew says the good soil represents the one who 'understands' the word (Matt. 13:23). Mark says the ones who 'hear the word and accept it' will bear fruit (Mark 4:20). Luke says the ones who 'hear the word, holding it fast' bear fruit with patience (Luke 8:15). Loving Jesus's words means we are listening to the Savior's voice, and hearing what He says to us.

The Apostle Peter used a different analogy: 'Like newborn infants, long for the pure spiritual milk, that by it you may grow up into salvation' (1 Pet. 2:2). In April 2014, we found a newborn whitetail fawn at Limerick, whose mother had died or abandoned him. He was at death's door, weak and dehydrated, unable to even lift his head. We quickly secured some goat's milk and put a few drops into his mouth with an eye dropper. Within minutes, a healthy pinkish color returned to his tongue, his nose became moist, and he hopped up and wobbled around the room. The immediate, life-giving effect of the milk made a profound impression. In fact, we named him 'Barnabas,' and he will always be an encouragement to me.

The words of Jesus are the spiritual milk, the source of sustenance for a life-giving relationship. The Apostle John, who was Christ's closest earthly friend, said, 'The Word became flesh, and dwelt among us, and we have seen his glory, glory as of the only Son from the Father, full of grace and truth … And from his grace we have all received, grace upon grace' (John 1:14, 16).

Putting down spiritual roots is not the result of an intellectual exercise, but the result of a new relationship. Kirsten Powers, a former Fox News commentator, described herself in a *Christianity Today* article as a 'highly reluctant Jesus follower.' Since college, Powers had been wavering between atheism and agnosticism, never coming close to considering that God could be real. Her unsought-after relationship with Christ began while she was attending church, at the invitation of her boyfriend. She remembers:

> I began to read the Bible. My boyfriend would pray with me for God to reveal himself to me. After about eight months … I concluded that the weight of evidence was on the side of Christianity. But I didn't feel any connection to God, and frankly, I was fine with that. I continued to think that people who talked of hearing from God or experiencing God were either delusional or lying. In my most generous moments, I allowed that they were just imagining things that made them feel good. Then one night in 2006, on a trip to Taiwan, I woke up in what felt like a strange cross between a dream and reality. Jesus came to me and said, 'Here I am.' It felt so real … I tried to write off the experience as misfiring synapses, but I couldn't shake it.[2]

On the advice of a friend, Kirsten joined a Bible study in New York, and this was her experience:

> I remember walking into the Bible study. I had a knot in my stomach. In my mind, only weirdos and zealots went to Bible studies. I don't remember what was said that day. All I know is that when I left, everything had changed. I'll never forget standing outside that apartment on the Upper East Side and saying to myself, 'It's true. It's completely true.' The world looked entirely different, like a veil had been lifted off it. I had not an iota of doubt. I was filled with indescribable joy.[3]

---

2. Kirsten Powers, *Christianity Today*, November 2013.
3. Ibid.

Every believer, no matter his or her intellectual capacity or level of education, has the tools to become a mature believer. Develop the habit, among other things, of daily communion with Christ and spending lots of time in the Word of God. The Apostle Peter reminds us that, 'His divine power has granted to us all things that pertain to life and godliness, through the knowledge of him who called us to his own glory and excellence, by which he has granted to us his precious and very great promises, so that through them you may become partakers of the divine nature' (2 Pet. 1:3-4). Remember, grace is the life of God at work in the soul of man. Planted in the soil of a healthy relationship with Christ, the seed cannot help but grow! Grace is not an attitude adjustment or a refined belief system, but a God-given power that transforms us.

Simply having religious interest or feelings does not free us from slavery to sin. Merely possessing a generic belief in the existence of God does not yield salvation. The gospel may be attractive to a person, but never take root. Faith may spring up quickly, and seem to flourish for a short season, but, without grace, it eventually fades away. I recently planted soybeans in a field, finishing the task in a heavy rain shower. A partial bag of seed had spilled in the front bucket of the tractor, and sat in warm water in the dark shed for a few days. The next time I pulled the tractor from the shed, I found the bucket full of inch-tall, ghastly-pale plants, with no soil and almost no roots!

Let your roots grow deeply into Christ, and build your entire life upon Him. Draw strength from His grace, and you will grow in His likeness. Changes may at times seem painfully imperceptible, but slow growth is growth.

GROWTH IS EXPECTED

Growing in grace is not merely desired by God – it is expected. Peter exhorts believers to 'make every effort to supplement your faith with virtue, and virtue with knowledge, and knowledge with self-control, and self-control with steadfastness, and steadfastness with godliness, and godliness with brotherly affection, and brotherly affection with love. For if these qualities are yours and are increasing, they keep you from being ineffective or unfruitful in the knowledge of our Lord Jesus Christ' (2 Pet. 1:5-8). Just as a parent expects his or her child to 'grow up' into a mature and self-sufficient adult, our heavenly Father expects His children to keep growing in grace. The Lord asked Isaiah pointedly, 'When I looked for [my vineyard] to yield grapes, why did it yield wild grapes?' (Isa. 5:4).

Unlike our physical bodies, which peak in maturity when we reach our 20s or early 30s, our spirits are capable of growing in grace all the way through old age until death. In fact, our declining physical capacities are frequently used by the Lord to stimulate spiritual growth. We will see more of that in the chapter on pruning. Whether by our design or by our default, decreasing self-reliance and increasing God-reliance is a powerful stimulant for sanctification. This is what the Psalmist calls going 'from strength to strength' (Ps. 84:7).

If an American alligator experiences fast growth early in life, followed by slow growth for the rest of its life, what is the typical growth pattern for a Christian believer? As we abide in Christ, our growth in grace is (i) usually slow, (ii) somewhat progressive, and (iii) always supernatural.

GROWTH IS USUALLY SLOW

Jesus told a parable about spiritual growth, warning His disciples that it is gradual. He said, 'The kingdom of God is as if a man should scatter seed on the ground. He sleeps and rises night and day, and the seed sprouts and grows; he knows not how. The earth produces by itself, first the blade, then the ear, then the full grain in the ear' (Mark 4:26-28). Experience bears this out. John Newton traced the contours of what he called the 'progressive work of grace' among the members of his congregation. The work of grace 'in the blade' describes a new believer. 'The beginning of this work is instantaneous. It is effected by a certain kind of light communicated to the soul, to which it was before an utter stranger. The eyes of understanding are opened and enlightened. The light at first afforded is weak and indistinct, like the morning dawn; but when it is once begun, it will certainly increase and spread to the perfect day.'[4] 'A tree is most valuable when laden with fruit, but it has a peculiar beauty when in blossom. It is spring-time with [him]; he is in bloom, and, by the grace and blessing of the heavenly husbandman, will bear fruit in old age.'[5]

Grace 'in the ear' describes the long, intermediate phase of spiritual growth which usually consumes most of our life. Such grace is 'of a growing nature, and is capable of increase so long as we remain in this world.'[6] Yet is remains marked by sin and frailty, perhaps with frequent trials and reversals. Growth in grace, though progressive, is not unfailingly upward in its trajectory.

There may be seasons of spiritual drought, perhaps caused by our withdrawal from fellowship with other believers or lack of good preaching and teaching. There may be seasons of withering oppression or frantic distraction. But, if we are rooted in Christ, spiritual vitality may falter but it will never be extinguished.

---

4. *Select Letters of John Newton*, p. 2.
5. Ibid., p. 6.
6. Ibid., p. 8.

We naturally want to rush the results. Diet commercials promise we can 'lose 30 pounds in 30 days.' But spiritual growth is a slow, almost imperceptible, phenomenon. The steady drip of Scripture transforms our thinking, alters our affections, and trains us in the unnatural skill of walking by faith. As we navigate life's circumstances and challenges by faith, God actively changes and refines us. Growth is a life-long process, in which the believer 'is like a tree planted by streams of water that yields its fruit in its season, and its leaf does not wither' (Ps. 1:3).

When a stand of mature timber is harvested, the place seems ugly and bare. Tree stumps, broken limbs, and deadfall are very unattractive. But in the coming months, early succession grasses, forbs (broad-leafed, non-woody plants), and shrubs (plants with woody stems) emerge, followed eventually by new trees. The slow growth of the trees over the next few decades transforms and restores the beauty of the landscape. Forestry is good spiritual training – it teaches patience with slow growth! The transferable concept of patiently tending a stand of timber with a 30 to 40 year life cycle is easily compared to a believer who walks with Christ through the seasons of life. It may seem imperceptible while it happens, but at the end when you look back, you realize it took place at a normal rate.

Like trees, individuals vary in growth rates. A pine tree takes 25 to 35 years to fully mature, depending on the amount of competition, nutrition, light and moisture it receives. An oak tree may take 50 to 75 years to mature. A Christian believer may take 40, 60, or 80 years to mature. It's all relative, in light of eternity. And why shouldn't it be slow? Growth is really a restoration of the way things ought to be, a slow reversal of the effects of the fall. Transformation rates vary with the intensity of the 'renewal of your mind' (Rom. 12:2), and as we 'put on the new self, which is being renewed' (Col. 3:10). The righteousness imparted to us at our new birth slowly yields a righteousness expressed in our life and character.

The image of a tree planted beside a stream of water in Psalm 1 means that the believer is constantly nourished and refreshed. Growth rings are added through the sequential progression of time. The tree yields its fruit in its season, and its leaf will not wither.

GROWTH IS *SOMEWHAT* STEADY

Notice in the parable of the growing seed that spiritual development in a believer is somewhat steady. 'Somewhat' is a relative term. Think about the U.S. stock market over the span of the century from 1920 to 2020. Viewed on a micro level, say in the decades between 1920 and 1930 or between 2000 and 2010, there were major declines and recessions. But viewed on a macro level, the overall progress has been generally upwards. So it is in the spiritual realm, as the believer 'sleeps and rises, night and day, and the seed sprouts and grows.'

John Newton described the growing believer this way:

> A depraved nature still cleaves to him, and he has the seeds of every natural corruption yet remaining in his heart. He lives likewise in a world that is full of snares and occasions, suited to draw forth those corruptions; and he is surrounded by invisible spiritual enemies, the extent of whose power and subtlety he is yet to learn from painful experience ... By a variety of these exercises, through the over-ruling and edifying influences of the Holy Spirit, (he) is trained up in a growing knowledge of himself and of the Lord.[7]

There will be regressions and setbacks along the way, but grace presses on.

---

7. *Select Letters of John Newton*, pp. 10, 12.

GROWTH IS ALWAYS SUPERNATURAL

The poorest soil can grow the richest crops, when supplemented with the right nutrients. Dr. Grant Woods is a biologist and avid outdoorsman who hosts a weekly on-line program, 'GrowingDeerTV.com.' Dr. Woods' central premise is that any soil, no matter how poor, can be amended and successfully cultivated. To test his theory, he purchased a very poor, rocky farm in Arkansas, and named it 'The Proving Grounds.' He says, 'We named the farm The Proving Grounds because this may be one of the harshest places in North America to hunt and "grow" mature whitetails. We thought that if the tools, practices and strategies we use here for growing and hunting whitetails succeed, they can work anywhere.'[8]

The rocky, nutrient-deprived terrain of The Proving Grounds has, in fact, produced rich crops and abundant wildlife. How did Woods manage it? With a lot of hard work: improving native browse with the use of prescribed fire, making timber stand improvements, and adding high-quality forage with his food plots. All of which translates into better, more plentiful nutrition for the wildlife. 'If it's not in the soil, it can't get to the deer,' Grant says.

In the same way, believers grow in grace through the steady, supernatural work of the Holy Spirit. Nothing more, and nothing less. We are powerless to produce true righteousness in ourselves. Yet, the divine power and influence of His Spirit is certain to change us. Attached to Christ, 'his divine power has granted to us all things that pertain to life and godliness, through the knowledge of him who called us to his own glory and excellence, by which he has granted to us his precious and very great promises, so that through them you may become

---

8. Grant Woods, GrowingDeerTV.com, 3/16/2018.

partakers of the divine nature' (2 Pet. 1:3-4). Peter is telling us that Christ alone can – and will – help us to grow.

One of the best definitions of grace is *help*. The author of Hebrews instructs us that we should 'with confidence draw near to the throne of grace, that we may receive mercy and find grace to help in time of need' (Heb. 4:16). If we want to grow in grace, we must look to Jesus. And He promises us to help all who turn to Him in faith: 'he helps the offspring of Abraham' (Heb. 2:16).

John Owen called the resulting grace which God produces in us 'habitual grace.' Such habitual grace is given to us to replace the principle of reigning sin that dominates us by nature. Owen said, 'In the understanding, it is light. In the will, it is obedience. In the affections, it is love. But it is all one principle, all one grace'[9]

Owen mirrors Paul's teaching that the Spirit helps us 'walk in him, rooted and built up in him, and established in your faith,' so that, by holding fast to Christ, the believer 'grows with a growth that is from God' (Col. 2: 6, 19). Purchased grace provides us habitual grace.

THE 'MEANS OF GRACE' – FERTILIZER FOR THE SOUL

Fertilizer is defined as any substance used to enrich the soil, making it more productive. Rudimentary forms of fertilizer include manure or other rotting biomass, such as compost or food scraps, that deliver supplemental nutrients to growing plants. More sophisticated (meaning, expensive!) fertilizers might be liquid or granular compounds, providing essential macronutrients such as nitrogen, phosphorus, and potassium, along with trace amounts of micronutrients, such as iron,

---

9. John Owen, *Communion With God*, p. 131.

manganese, and boron. As we said earlier, fertilizer labeled '10-10-10' contains 10% nitrogen (N), 10% phosphorus (P), and 10% potassium (K) by volume. Therefore, one hundred pounds of 10-10-10 contains ten pounds of nitrogen, ten pounds of phosphorus, and ten pounds of potassium. Farmers often add as much as 200 to 300 pounds of fertilizer per acre when planting corn, soybeans, or other crops, and later supplement it with another 100 to 200 pounds of pure nitrogen (34-0-0) per acre when the plants begin to mature. It often takes a lot of fertilizer to produce healthy crops!

How effective is fertilizer? I recently conducted a simple experiment. In a cow pasture, I applied several bags of 34-0-0 fertilizer in alternating strips, leaving gaps several yards wide. A week or two later, I came back and the strips of fertilized grass were dark green, and had grown noticeably taller than the unfertilized grass. Same soil, same amounts of rain and sun, yet the contrast was profound. So, are you consistently fertilizing your soul to grow in grace?

Historically, pastors and theologians have found in Scripture three primary ways in which believers are helped to grow in grace: (i) the preaching of the Word, (ii) prayer, and (iii) the sacraments of baptism and the Lord's Supper. These seemingly ordinary (even mundane!) things are God-given aids for spiritual growth. They are the main ways God's people grow. Let's look at each one more closely.

The Word of God. When a farmer plants seeds with a mechanical planter or grain drill, the device digs a trench, drops the seed, and closes the hole, all in one pass through the field. The depth of planting, to assure good contact with the soil, is crucial. A problem arises with small grains, such as wheat, oats, clover, rye, or millet, which are merely sown on the surface. How can the planter assure good seed-to-soil contact? Often, he will go back over the field with a drag to lightly cover the seed, or roll over it with a 'cultipacker' to press the seed into the soil, improving soil contact. Without good soil contact, germination rates are low, and predation by birds and other critters is very high.

The same principle applies with the seed of the Word of God. It must be planted in our hearts and minds, or it will not germinate. Merely reading or hearing the Scriptures read is like top-sowing; some of the seed will sprout, but much of it will be snatched by predators or just lie dormant on the surface. Hearing or reading a detailed explanation of the text, however, is like a farmer using a planter, grain drill, or cultipacker. It plants the seed more firmly in our hearts.

Preaching is simply the expounding of the Word of God. In Old Testament Israel, the prophet Ezra called the people to gather as a congregation, and he and the priests 'read from the book, from the Law of God, clearly, and they gave the sense, so that the people understood the reading' (Neh. 8:8). The Apostle Paul used the same approach wherever he preached the gospel: 'I did not shrink from declaring to you anything that was profitable, and teaching you in public and from house to house, testifying both to Jews and to Greeks of repentance toward God and of faith in our Lord Jesus Christ' (Acts 20:20-21). Expounding, applying, testifying to the reliability of the scriptures, Paul 'sowed it thick,' and it yielded a rich harvest.

As nitrogen is the primary building block for plant protein, so Scripture is the primary building block for our souls. God explicitly instructs His people to 'devote yourself to the public reading of Scripture, to exhortation, to teaching' (1 Tim. 4:13). Pastors are told to 'preach the word; be ready in season and out of season; reprove, rebuke, and exhort, with complete patience and teaching' (2 Tim. 4:2). The regular intake of Scripture, both in personal study and devotional reading, as well as in corporate gatherings, such as Sunday worship and group Bible studies, is vital. We cannot over-emphasize the primary role of Scripture for our growth in grace. Jesus prayed for His followers in His final hours, asking that His Father in heaven would 'sanctify them in the truth; your word is truth' (John 17:17).

Reading and hearing the exposition of God's Word should not be a passive activity. The key concept to understand is that the Word itself is 'living and active, sharper than any two-edged sword' (Heb. 4:12). It 'performs its work in you believers' (1 Thess. 2:13). God's voice actively speaks to us through Scripture: 'So shall my word be that goes out from my mouth; it shall not return to me empty, but it shall accomplish that which I purpose, and shall succeed in the thing for which I sent it' (Isa. 55:11). Like yeast in a warm lump of dough, or mother's milk for a hungry infant, or fertilizer on a growing plant, the living word is the change agent which causes something 'supernatural' to happen. It infuses life into the recipient.

We should view every Bible reading and every sermon as a private counseling session with God's Spirit. Allow the silent sound of His voice to instruct, to encourage, to challenge, to warn us. Ask the Lord to give clear understanding, and to provide spiritual strength to receive and act upon the words given. The Bible calls this 'having ears to hear and eyes to see.' Without the earphones connected, we can't hear anything!

Beyond reading the word of God, the detailed study of it is transformative. Learn to study Scripture on your own, with or without the use of 'study aids' such as commentaries, books (such as this one!), devotionals, and other sources. To learn the outline of a book of the Bible, to memorize a few key verses or chapters, to roll it over and over in your mind, meditating on the meaning and application of the text to your life and circumstances – all of these are like a cow chewing its cud. Rumination aids in the digestion and assimilation of God's truth into our thoughts, words and actions. Scripture transforms us and renews our mind (Rom. 12:2). It changes our thinking, elevates our perspective, focuses our priorities, and produces fruit in our lives. By its irrepressible power, 'the word of truth, the gospel ... is bearing fruit and growing – as it does among you, since the day you heard it and understood the grace of God in truth' (Col. 1:5-6). Scripture intake is the primary means by which God infuses grace into our souls.

Prayer. The second 'means of grace' is prayer. Again, this includes both private prayer as well as public prayers offered when the church family is together. The Apostle Paul instructed the churches, 'I urge that supplications, prayers, intercessions, and thanksgivings be made ... I desire that in every place men should pray, lifting holy hands' (1 Tim. 2:1). Prayer is neither an empty meditation (thinking about nothing, to clear the mind) nor a rambling list of formulaic words and petitions. It is a thoughtful, humble, exchange – both speaking and listening – between the Creator and His creature. In talking to God, believers are encouraged to 'draw near to the throne of grace, that we may receive mercy and find grace to help in time of need' (Heb. 4:16).

What makes the difference in prayer? Coming to the Father on the basis of our relationship with His son. Approaching God is, in a sense, like logging into a computer network, to communicate with someone. If we try to enter it without a password, we are denied access. Our sin has corrupted us and made our requests unrecognizable. But if we enter in Jesus' name, using His credentials, we are given direct access to the Father. The logic behind our access to God is that Christ, our divine host, has invited us into the meeting: 'For Christ has entered, not into holy places made with hands ... but into heaven itself, now to appear in the presence of God on our behalf' (Heb. 9:24).

Prayer is simply talking to God. Yet there are certain 'how to' lessons Jesus taught His followers that are useful. First, we must find an undistracted time of solitude ('go into your room and shut the door'). Second, there should be a rhythm of both speaking and silence ('do not heap up empty phrases as the Gentiles do, for they think that they will be heard for their many words'). Third, our words and requests are best marked by simplicity ('pray then like this: "Our Father in heaven, hallowed be your name."'). Fourth, there is a basic structure of topics to be addressed, in order of importance ('your name,' 'your kingdom,' 'your will,' 'our daily bread,' etc.). And, finally, there must be a basic sincerity in seeking God's favor ('if you forgive others their trespasses, your heavenly Father will also forgive you'). See Christ's entire exposition on the basics of prayer in Matthew 6:5-18. To pray effectively, we need a quiet place, a quiet hour, and a quiet heart – all three of which can be extremely challenging to find!

Many find it helpful periodically to write out their prayers. In fact, most of the Psalms are written prayers, converted into songs for meditation and worship. The act of writing is useful because writing focuses our thinking. And it gives us a permanent record of prayers made and answered, as a further encouragement to perseverance in prayer.

Most private prayer is done silently, but nothing in the Bible says it should be done that way. Many find it helpful to speak aloud to the Lord, literally asking the Lord to 'give attention to the sound of my cry ... in the morning you hear my voice' (Ps. 5:2, 3). Speaking aloud to God not only keeps our minds from wandering as readily, but it also creates the feel of a personal conversation with a trusted friend, our loving Father and Savior.

Few believers have the kind of memory or ability to focus that allows them to be a skillful pray-er without some kind of journal, notebook, or other system for organization. Feel free to experiment with a three-ring binder, a spiral-bound or leather-bound journal, a card system (which I like), or simply a stack of written reminders (which my friend, Dr. Douglas Kelly uses) to keep yourself on track. Write out prayers and scripture passages, and read them aloud. Eventually, the pattern of words becomes engrained in our minds and takes root in our hearts. Intentionality in prayer is as important as intentionality in keeping up with a friend. If you don't plan it, it usually won't happen!

Sacraments. The third 'means of grace' is the regular observation of the sacraments – both baptism and the Lord's Supper. These acts of God-ordained ceremony serve as a visual reminder – an acted-out parable – of what God has graciously done for His people. In baptism, we see a visual depiction of the washing away of our sins. In the Lord's Supper, we see and receive tangible reminders that the body and blood of Christ were offered as a perfect sacrifice for our transgressions. The former is prescribed in Scripture as a one-time event for each believer (Acts 2:38). The latter is to be repeated often (1 Cor. 11:25). The symbolism of the sacraments alone is powerful, but the practical effect of sincere, humble, regular observation of the sacraments is transformative, keeping us near the Savior, and growing us in His grace.

A useful habit during the celebration of the Lord's Supper is to focus specifically on Christ seated at the right hand of the Father, with all dominion, power, and authority. Praise Him for His beauty and strength, thank Him for His atoning sacrifice, look forward expectantly to seeing His glory, and yearn for the fellowship with Him when we hear the blessed words, 'Well done, good and faithful servant; enter into your Master's rest.' The Lord's Supper is best celebrated looking forward to Christ's heavenly companionship as much as looking back at

His earthly ministry, though both aspects of His completed work are profound and rich.

Though Scripture does not tell us how often to take communion or provide other detailed instructions (real wine or grape juice?), it is clear that the ceremony is a real-time visit with the risen Savior. Paul invites us to cultivate a sense of entering into Christ's presence at the table: 'The cup of blessing that we bless, is it not a participation in the blood of Christ? The bread that we break, is it not a participation in the body of Christ?' (1 Cor. 10:16). The mysterious union and communion we share with the Lord around His table is fertilizer for the soul. Why would any believer neglect this extraordinary means of grace?

THE GOAL IS MATURITY IN CHRIST

Mature, healthy crops are impressive. Tall, lush, green, and laden with fruit, they speak volumes about the skill and diligence of the farmer. Maturity doesn't just happen!

So it is in the spiritual realm. The Lord's goal for every believer is that he or she become mature and produce much fruit. The Apostle Paul described his ministry in these terms: 'Him we proclaim, warning everyone and teaching everyone with all wisdom, that we may present everyone mature in Christ' (Col. 1:28). To be mature in Christ means that we are so deeply connected to Him that He begins to rub off on us. Jesus put it bluntly: 'Whoever abides in me and I in him, he it is that bears much fruit, for apart from me you can do nothing' (John 15:5).

Connection to Jesus is the key. He alone is the One 'through whom we have received grace … to bring about the obedience of faith' (Rom. 1:5). In our struggles with sin, we should focus less on ourselves (our obedience, our feelings, our attitudes) and focus more on Jesus and His grace, His forgiveness, His all-sufficiency. We are called to be strong, not in ourselves, but in the grace that is in Jesus.

Maturity in Christ means having 'clearer, deeper, and more comprehensive views of the mystery of redeeming love; of the glorious excellency of the Lord Jesus, in his person, offices, grace, and faithfulness; of the harmony and glory of all the divine perfections manifested in and by him to the church.'[10] For the mature believer, 'his great business is to behold the glory of God in Christ; and by beholding, he is changed into the same image, and brings forth in an eminent and uniform manner the fruits of righteousness, which are by Jesus Christ to the glory and praise of God.'[11]

Ironically, it is in knowing how vile my heart is, how prone I am to wander from the path, and realizing how utterly dependent I am upon Him to keep me from falling, that I gain a sense of my own insufficiency. Then, and only then, does the grip of sin begin to lose its sway over us, and the clearer focus of our prayers, plans, and actions becomes the enjoyment and honoring of our precious Savior. The mature believer 'is the object and residence of divine love, the charge of angels, and ripening for everlasting joy.'[12]

A basic skill for every believer to learn is routinely preaching the gospel to yourself. We should practice Spirit-guided 'cognitive behavior therapy,' telling ourselves over and over the truths of Scripture. Dr. Derek Thomas has said that, within minutes of waking daily, as he gains consciousness, he repeats, 'Nothing in my hands I bring; simply to Thy cross I cling.'

Maturity in Christ will never be fully realized in this life. Yet grace, by God's power, is capable of growing as long as we are alive. Such growth occurs unevenly, in fits and starts, and with

---

10. John Newton, *Select Letters of John Newton,* p. 15.

11. Ibid, p. 15.

12. Ibid. p. 20.

occasional setbacks. But it grows, nevertheless, as Isaiah said, 'that they may be called oaks of righteousness, the planting of the LORD, that he may be glorified' (Isa. 61:3).

Grace produces the growth.

5

THE WEEDS

'For sin will have no dominion over you, since you are not under law but under grace' (Rom. 6:14).

Dr. Marshall McGlamery, a retired horticulturalist from the University of Illinois, once defined a weed as 'any plant whose virtues are unknown, but whose vices are.'[1] Some weeds are merely a nuisance, competing with crops for light, nutrients, and moisture. Others are noxious, not only competing with, but overwhelming, the good plants. Sicklepod, foxtail, horsenettle, cocklebur, pigweed, and johnsongrass, are deep-rooted, aggressive weeds that can doom a farmer. Economic loss, ecological harm, human or animal injury, or just plain ugliness of the landscape may result, unless they are destroyed.

Fortunately, there are many ways to fight weeds: chemical herbicides, both pre-emergent and post-emergent; mechanical

---

1. W. Carroll Johnson III, *Quality Food Plots*, Quality Deer Management Association, 2006, p. 152.

weed control, such as mowing, digging, or plowing; prescribed fire; or simply planting crops with rapid growth rates, to outpace the weeds. A farm consultant once recommended that I spray a weed-infested field with herbicide, then burn the withered plants, then plow them under, and then wait a few months, and do it all over again! As the old saying goes, 'It is not enough for a gardener to love flowers. He must also hate the weeds!'

Weed control is a war, and winning the war starts with a crucial piece of information: know your enemy. Scripture warns us that the spiritual weeds infesting our hearts are (i) common in every one, (ii) competitors to the good seed, (iii) potentially catastrophic, but (iv) by grace, controllable.

COMMON

The weeds of sin are universal to all mankind. Just like natural weeds, they exist everywhere, without exception. In the natural world, find a field or pasture that is weed-free, and you can bet it has been treated or cultivated. Weed-free ground does not exist naturally, without human intervention.

So it is in the spiritual realm. The sinful nature we inherited from our first parents, Adam and Eve, has infested all mankind. No one is without sin. No, not one. We may recoil at the charge that we are born sinners, but the proof is evident in our lives. Dr. Douglas Kelly of Reformed Theological Seminary in Charlotte, North Carolina, tells of being accosted by a dignified, but outraged, woman after a church service. 'Who are you calling a sinner? I'm a fine, Southern woman!' Genteel manners and social graces aside, each of us harbors a heart of darkness. From the gross sins to the more respectable sins, we all display shocking degrees of pride, varieties of lust, and a selfish life focus. Uncontrolled, the wild seed grows and produces its own fruit. The Apostle Paul issues an indictment that stands: 'Now the works of the flesh are evident: sexual immorality, impurity, sensuality, idolatry, sorcery, enmity, strife, jealousy, fits of anger, rivalries, dissensions, divisions, envy, drunkenness, orgies, and things like these' (Gal. 5:19-20). A thought becomes a word; a word becomes an action; an action becomes a habit; and a habit condemns us. From the temper tantrums of self-willed toddlers to the more subtle transgressions of sophisticated adults, the evidence is clear. And these noxious weeds are common to all.

Scripture uses three key words to describe sin. A side-by-side comparison is found in Psalm 51:1-2, where David wrote, 'Be gracious to me, O God, according to your steadfast mercy, blot out my *transgressions*, wash me thoroughly from my *iniquity*, and cleanse me from my *sin*!' To 'transgress' means to step over the line; to go too far. To commit 'iniquity' means to twist, pervert or deform something from its original shape or design, such as profane speech or sexual immorality. To 'sin' means to fall short; to fail to honor God as Creator; to not do as we know we ought to do. By using this triad of terms – three separate, but related words – David was emphasizing the completeness of his depravity. And I am no different! Let me illustrate.

In 2016 I was bow-hunting elk in Meeker, Colorado, with my son, Bryan. Never having seen an elk before, I was startled when I crested a ridge the first day and saw a huge bull elk standing broadside in an open field, staring at me. I had no time to grab my rangefinder to measure the yardage, so I guessed the bull was 40 yards away (though, in fact, he was only 30 yards away) and shot the arrow. It sailed cleanly over his back. That was like a 'transgression' – the arrow went too far. Transgressors cross the line – we *disobey* God's word and do the things He forbids.

The elk ran a short distance, startled but unscathed, then stopped to look back. Hurrying, I guessed the elk was now at 50 yards (though in fact the distance was 55 yards) and let another arrow fly. The missile landed harmlessly at his feet. That was like a 'sin' – the arrow fell short. Sinners fall short of God's moral requirements – we *distrust* God's commands, not doing what He instructs.

Frustrated with the missed shot opportunities, let's just say my speech was not seasoned with grace. That was 'iniquity' – misusing words and speech (or anything else God intended to be used for His glory or the good of others). Iniquiters twist and pervert what is good – we *distort* God's ways, abusing or marring the image of God in us.

Farmers must be as adept at identifying weeds as they are at recognizing good plants. Some noxious or invasive weeds are obvious, like horsethistle, but often the differences can be very subtle. Certain weeds look benign until they mature, when it is too late to spray, burn, or pull them, for fear of harming the good crop. That was the point of Jesus's parable about the tares (undesirable weeds) and the wheat (desirable crop) in Matthew 13. An invasive weed we call 'coffeebean' looks very similar to a soybean plant when it first emerges. But the imposter is poisonous.

Often, I admit, I have trouble distinguishing the good plants from the bad plants in my fields. So I use an app called 'Picture This' to identify any grass or plant that looks suspicious. Can you identify the weeds in the garden of your heart? The Holy Spirit will help to reveal the ungodly thoughts, motives, and attitudes that are deeply rooted in us. He gives grace to see them for what they are – worthless and destructive.

We may strongly dislike or even resent the doctrine of original sin, but we all have to admit there are weeds in our garden. We routinely overstep God's boundaries, fall short of God's righteous requirements, and pursue all kinds of iniquity. As Paul said, 'All have sinned and fall short of the glory of God' (Rom. 3:23).

From the most noxious sins, such as murder, adultery, lying, and stealing, to the more common and (seemingly) harmless varieties, such as malice, deceit, hypocrisy, envy, and slander, 'whatever overcomes a person, to that he is enslaved' (2 Pet. 2:19). Our attitudes, thoughts, motives, words, and actions and motives are universally overgrown with weeds.

COMPETITORS

At regeneration, the Spirit plants the seed of righteousness in our hearts. By grace, that seed begins to take root and grow. But the sin which is already established clings tenaciously to its ground. The remnants of our old, sinful nature remain at odds with the new nature, and those weeds never surrender easily. The battle is on between our old self (the flesh) and the new self (the Spirit). This never-ending struggle frustrates and confounds even the most committed believer. Even the Apostle Paul said, 'I do not understand my actions. For I do not do what I want, but I do the very thing I hate ... For I have the desire to do what is right, but not the ability to carry it out' (Rom. 7: 15, 18).

Apart from God's grace, there would be no effective means of killing the weeds. Self-help is ineffective. God alone can reach into our hearts and destroy the tap root of sin, by the blood of Christ. He gradually gives believers freedom from the power of sin. This transformation begins with *convicting grace*. The Holy Spirit quickens our conscience, removes the veil from our eyes, and makes us understand the horror of our sin. Only then by grace can we turn humbly to God for help. 'For the grace of God has appeared ... training us to renounce ungodliness and worldly passions, and to live self-controlled, upright and godly lives in the present age' (Titus 2:11-12). Convicting grace is like an herbicide to destroy the weeds.

John Newton was first drawn to Christ in 1748, while serving, ironically, as the captain's mate of a slave ship, the *Brownlow*. Plying the seas between Great Britain, Africa, and the Americas, he was an active participant in the capture, bondage, and sale of African slaves. During the voyages, he would abuse the slaves, beating the men and sexually molesting the women. The dominance of his anger and the habits of his lust before becoming a Christian believer lingered, even after he made a public profession of faith in Christ, was baptized, joined a church, and started a daily pattern of devotional readings! Newton wrote, 'I followed a course of evil, which a few months before I should not have supposed myself any longer capable ... I had little desire and no power to recover myself.'[2] The reality that he was a slave to his own sin terrified him. He lamented, 'The enemy prepared a train of temptations, and I became his easy prey.'[3] Many years later, he wrote the famous hymn which takes on new meaning in light of his admitted conduct:

'Amazing grace, how sweet the sound,
that saved a wretch like me.
I once was lost, but now I am found;
was blind, but now I see.'

But Newton's hymn also sheds light on the work of convicting grace:

'Tis grace that taught my heart to fear,
and grace my fears relieved.
How precious did that grace appear,
the hour I first believed.'

Ask the Lord for convicting grace.

---

2. *From Disgrace to Grace*, p. 93.
3. Ibid., p. 94.

POTENTIALLY CATASTROPHIC

A common misconception among believers is the idea that because God loves me and Christ died to cover the guilt of my sin, it does not matter how I live. Once saved, always saved, right? Or worse, we might foolishly think that our ongoing sin actually adds more glory to God, because it proves how merciful He is. The grave danger in this mindset is that a sinful, weed-filled life dishonors God and begs the question of whether the person was ever converted in the first place. Paul asks, 'Are we to continue in sin that grace may abound? By no means! How can we who died to sin still live in it?' (Rom. 6:1-2). The grace-filled soul longs for true righteousness, not wanting to live on the edge of catastrophe. If we cherish our sin more deeply than we cherish our Savior, the cares of the world and the deceitfulness of riches will eventually choke the spiritual life out of us. Oh, the danger of clinging to the sin which so easily entangles us.

For the nonbeliever, sin is not merely a distraction: it dominates life and actually enslaves the sinner. This is called *total depravity*. Never content to be our servant, sin becomes our master. Paul puts it bluntly: 'For when you were slaves to sin … what fruit were you getting at that time from the things of which you are now ashamed? For the end of those things is death' (Rom. 6:21). The natural hunger for the riches, cares and pleasures of the world (Luke 8:14), takes over, destroying the life of the sinner. If the weeds win the battle for space, sunlight, moisture, and nutrients from the soil, they inevitably kill the crop.

As I write these words, I am looking out the window at a lush hay field at the foot of the Bitterroot Mountains in western Montana. The owner has placed a sign on the gate entering his property: 'POSTED. NO TRESPASSING.' It is a harsh warning, with the symbol of a video camera, but it's clear he intends to protect his turf. In the same way, Scripture warns us of the danger of remaining in sin. It is possible for a person to be interested in spiritual things, attracted to Christ, and yet allow or even nurture the very weeds that will destroy their faith. Left unchecked, the weeds can reach a tipping point, where they overwhelm the good seed. Peter urges believers to 'abstain from the passions of the flesh, which wage war against your soul' (1 Pet. 2:11).

In fact, in many ways the constant struggle against sin is more frustrating after turning to Christ, because we know how offensive it is to our Father in heaven. Behaviors and habits which once infatuated us and made us feel good for a moment, now come with a greater load of guilt and shame. Yet, we may also want to cling to our sin because we enjoy it. Worldliness is the desire to keep a few weeds in the garden, for fun. But the toys can become traps. James warns us: 'What causes quarrels and what causes fights among you? Is it not this, that your passions are at war within you? You desire and do not have, so you murder. You covet and cannot obtain, so you fight and quarrel … You adulterous people! Do you not know that friendship with the world is enmity with God?' (James 4:1-2, 4). One of the keys to the Christian walk is prayerful introspection. Ask God for grace to see the horror of your sin. A worldly Christian is like a weed-infested field. O God, why do all these weeds keep emerging in my heart?

Every believer should develop a healthy fear of sin. To know the free offer of the gospel, yet to harbor a love for the illicit pleasures and destructive pastimes of this world, leaves us in a very dangerous position. Paul admonishes us: 'For land that has drunk the rain that often falls on it, and produces a crop useful to those for whose sake it is cultivated, receives a blessing from God. But if it bears thorns and thistles, it is worthless and near to being cursed, and its end is to be burned' (Heb. 6:7-8).

Run from it! 'Abhor what is evil; hold fast to what is good' (Rom. 12:9).

The worldly believer is in grave danger of succumbing to the weeds in his life. Heed the notice: 'See to it that no one fails to obtain the grace of God, that no root of bitterness springs up and causes trouble, and by it many become defiled; that no one is sexually immoral or unholy like Esau, who sold his birthright for a single meal' (Heb. 12:15-16). Left unchecked, the weeds will overtake the wheat: 'For whatever one sows, that he will also reap. For the one who sows to his own flesh will from the flesh reap corruption, but the one who sows to the Spirit will from the Spirit reap eternal life' (Gal. 6:7-8). Do not sow weeds in your own garden!

We are cautioned in Scripture not to quench the Spirit by consciously ignoring or resisting His warnings. The restraining power of the Spirit, which nudges our conscience with a sense of guilt when we overstep, can become seared. Violated or ignored long enough, it ceases to function.

The good news of the gospel is that grace gives the believer the power to overcome sin. The blood of Christ breaks the tap root of sin, and it no longer proliferates, uncontrolled.

CONTROLLABLE

In the 1970s, the Monsanto Company patented a game-changing herbicide under the tradename 'Round Up.' The active ingredient in Round Up is the potent chemical glyphosate, a post-emergent, broad-spectrum herbicide which destroys a plant from the leaves down to the root. It works by stopping photosynthesis, so the plant cannot absorb energy from the sunlight, and the plant withers within hours of spraying. Round Up has been so commercially successful that its name has become an eponym; its name is synonymous with its purpose.

When Round Up first appeared on the market, it was a blessing for farmers. Simply spraying the weeds saves hours of difficult work, instead of the tedious job of pulling or plowing them. But a new dilemma arose. Once the planted crops began to grow, Round Up could not be re-applied, because it killed every plant it touched, both the good and the bad. Then the real game-changer came when seed companies developed Round Up-resistant crops, such as corn or soybeans. So-called 'Round Up Ready' seeds were genetically engineered for immunity to glyphosate, increasing yields by destroying only the moisture- and nutrient-sucking weeds.

Aside from agricultural uses, herbicides also have wonderful applications around the home. Weeds in the flower bed? No problem! Grab a sprayer and squirt the weeds – psst, psst, psst – and they are gone. Weeds in the cracks of your sidewalk? No problem! Psst, psst, psst, and they are gone.

What if we could do the same with sin? We cannot, but grace can. One of the effects of grace is that it destroys the dominion of sin over the soul that is in Christ. Grace works its way down into the tap root of sin, cutting off its deep supply of nutriments and moisture. The blood of Christ is the only agent that destroys sin. The mortification of sin, as it is called, is a long, slow process. But it begins the moment we are united to Christ by faith.

Not to sound trite, but let's say a Christian believer still has a habit of mean, critical thoughts toward others. The initial work of grace is to disturb his or her conscience, warning that such pride or hatred is sinful. The Holy Spirit applies 'Grace Up' and psst, psst, psst, it is gone. (Warning: weeds are likely to re-appear, and must be sprayed again and again, until eventually eradicated.) Lust? Pride? Anger? Greed? Laziness? Use Grace Up! A few years ago, one of my young granddaughters was having a very bad, whiny morning. Her mother said, 'Eliza

Ann, you are being ugly and selfish.' The two-year old said, 'Pray Jesus, happy heart.' In a childish way, she got the concept.

Round Up is applied to weeds with a sprayer. Grace Up is applied with confession of sin, through prayer. As James explains it, 'Draw near to God, and he will draw near to you. Cleanse your hands, you sinners, and purify your hearts, you double-minded ... Humble yourselves before the Lord, and he will exalt you' (James 4:8, 10). We must learn to run to Jesus quickly when we sin, honestly confessing our shame and guilt, asking Him to forgive and cleanse us.

An interesting fact about Round Up is that it works best if the farmer adds a small amount of 'surfactant,' such as common household detergent, to the mixture. The surfactant reduces the surface tension of the oily coating on a plant's leaves, allowing the glyphosate to enter the plant more easily and work more quickly. (This is the same reason handwashing is effective in destroying germs. Soap does not merely wash germs away, but the soap molecules actually break down the lipid membrane of the bacteria or virus, disarming its defenses. Many pathogens, including coronaviruses and the viruses that cause Ebola, hepatitis B and C, and numerous bacteria, are no match for common soap!) A sensitive conscience and a contrite heart, which lead quickly to the confession of sin, are the believer's surfactant. We should confess sin as habitually as we wash our hands! One of the most encouraging promises in Scripture is found in Romans 6:14: 'For sin will have no dominion over you, since you are not under law but under grace.'

God graciously and patiently helps the believer weed out sin. The slow process of growing in grace is called 'sanctification' or the 'mortification of sin.' It means being less and less drawn into sinful patterns of thought, speech, and conduct, and gradually becoming more obedient in all our ways. The new believer wakes up the day of his conversion, so to speak, with the same personality, the same habits, and the same flaws he had before his new birth. Outwardly, he looks the same, but a new spirit has been placed within him, which will eventually change his affections and transform his ways. The change, though radical, may not yet be visible.

When a farmer sprays Round Up or other herbicides on his fields, the change is not instantly noticeable. The weeds show no signs of damage until hours, or even days, later. In fact, I often marvel while spraying that, with a light sheen of mist from the sprayer on their leaves, the weeds appear healthier and stronger than ever. But they are as good as dead!

Another reality in the battle against weeds is that it often takes several growing seasons to see real progress. Why? I might spray a field this year, killing all visible weeds, only to find the next year after plowing and planting that I have another infestation of the same weed. The seeds of the noxious plant were still in the seedbank of the soil. But eventually, after successive rounds, the weeds are brought under control. So it is in the life of the believer. Weeds that we thought were eradicated from our life long ago may re-emerge. Don't lose heart. Hit them again. Persevere in mortifying sin, and the victory will come. Paul encourages us, 'Do not be overcome by evil, but overcome evil with good' (Rom. 12:21).

How does a believer grow in grace and make progress in the mortification of sin?

Confess your sin. Make it a habit to go quickly and frequently to God, asking for His forgiveness. The grace that comes with sincere repentance is profound. God promises, 'For I will be merciful toward their iniquities, and I will remember their sins no more' (Heb. 8:12). Not only should we confess our sins to God, but also confess our sins to one another, asking the person we may have offended for forgiveness and reconciliation. The Lord tramples down our iniquities, not merely pardoning us from guilt, but eventually releasing us from the power of sin. True liberation comes only when Christ breaks the power of sin that holds us. See Romans 6:6, 14. Sometimes this happens dramatically, and at other times liberation is a long, slow process. But freedom comes by grace: 'For the law of the Spirit of life has set you free in Christ Jesus from the law of sin and death' (Rom. 8:2). Pull the weeds while they are small!

Know what sin looks like, and know how much it both displeases the Father and harms the child. This self-awareness comes from the discipline of healthy introspection, aided by looking closely in the mirror of Scripture. Ask the Lord to give you a sensitive conscience, which convicts you of sin immediately. Scripture warns against callousness toward sin: 'For if we go on sinning deliberately after receiving the knowledge of the truth, there no longer remains a sacrifice for sins' (Heb. 10:26).

Confess sins of motive, thought, word and deed as soon as they occur. Plead with God as the psalmist did: 'Have mercy on me, O God, according to your steadfast love; according to your abundant mercy, blot out my transgressions' (Ps. 51:1). 'God is opposed to the proud, but gives grace to the humble' (I Pet. 5:5).

<u>Pray for new affections</u>. Scripture calls this 'walking by the Spirit,' as we will see more closely in the next chapter. Minute by minute, as we consciously live in the presence of the Savior, He gently leads us in paths of righteousness for His name's sake. Paul says that where our mind and heart are focused, our hands and feet will follow: 'For those who live according to the flesh set their minds on the things of the flesh, but those who live according to the Spirit set their minds on the things of the Spirit. For to set the mind on the flesh is death, but to set the mind on the Spirit is life and peace' (Rom. 8:5-6). Part of walking by the Spirit is recognizing and avoiding patterns

of behavior or certain relationships that lead us astray. Don't intentionally sow weeds in your own garden. A friend used to tell me, 'If you want to hunt ducks, go where the ducks are.' The spiritual corollary is, 'If you want to avoid sin, don't go where the temptation is.'

Ask the Lord to take away the taste for sin, and to grant you a stronger thirst for righteousness. He promises to help those who hunger and thirst for obedience: 'For the grace of God has appeared ... training us to renounce ungodliness and worldly passions, and to live self-controlled, upright and godly lives' (Titus 2:11-12). Ask Him for grace to become a slave of righteousness (Rom. 6:18).

The battle against sin is spiritual in nature. Plead with the Lord for deliverance from evil and for the grace of self-control. Short, frequent, and fervent petitions are generally more effective than long, protracted, wearisome efforts. We are not heard for our many words. Peter, who failed often but kept walking with God, assures us: 'The God of all grace, who has called you to his eternal glory in Christ, will himself restore, confirm, strengthen and establish you' (1 Pet. 5:10).

<u>Study and meditate on Scripture</u>. As we have seen, Scripture is a change agent. It transforms our thinking, which alters our conduct. Paul underscores the power of the Word to change us: 'Be transformed by the renewal of your mind, that by testing you may discern what is the will of God, what is good and acceptable and perfect' (Rom. 12:2). This change is slow and almost imperceptible, but it is also inevitable. Elsewhere, we are told that rather than being 'unskilled in the word of righteousness,' we should have our 'powers of discernment trained by constant practice to distinguish good from evil' (Heb. 5:13, 14).

The grace of life is found only in the Word of Life. Steep yourself in His words. 'If you abide in me, and my words abide in you, ask whatever you wish, and it will be done for you' (John 15:7). Sow the word as thick as you can.

Surround yourself with one or two fellow believers who know you well, and give them freedom to ask you the hard questions, and to hold you accountable.

Take full advantage of the 'means of grace' on a regular basis. Devotion to hearing the preached word, participation in the public sacraments, and gathering for corporate prayer are powerful means, given by God, for our spiritual growth. The means of grace are like a surfactant to facilitate and accelerate the sin-destroying power of grace.

Devote yourself to service. An interesting thing happens when we pour time, energy and resources into serving others. We become less self-focused and more content to dwell in whatever field God has planted us. Grace grows as we put our hand to the plow.

At the end of the day, our salvation and sanctification depend entirely on God's grace. Unless we are firmly gripped and sustained by His grace, there is no limit to the depths to which we might fall. But His grace is utterly dependable, and we may stand firmly in it.

THE LONG WAIT

Every farmer knows that the time between planting and harvest takes patience. A corn crop takes at least 90 days to mature, and some varieties take as long as 120 days. Young grape vines planted from seeds usually take several years to begin producing fruit. 'See how the farmer waits for the precious fruit of the earth, being patient about it, until it receives the early and the late rains. You also, be patient. Establish your hearts, for the coming of the Lord is at hand' (James 5:7-8). When the harvest finally arrives, the season of preparing and planting seems like a distant memory. So it can be with our sanctification. It is a long, slow process, with frequent setbacks and challenges along the way.

Like a seasoned farmer, the Lord works patiently to cultivate the crop. Along the way, He must deal with the weeds in the lives of His children. But the Lord has a variety of strategies to manage the weeds:

1. **Destruction.** The farmer may commit an all-out assault on the weeds at the start of the season. Burning, mowing, plowing, and spraying the weeds certainly do a number on them. 'Put to death what is earthly in you: sexual immorality, impurity, passion, evil desire, and covetousness, which is idolatry' (Col. 3:5). Sometimes, drastic measures have to be taken to eradicate noxious sin in our lives. Ending bad relationships, dropping harmful habits, walking away from known sources of temptation. The point is to break the tap root of sin, so that it no longer holds a place of dominion. This destruction only comes by grace. 'He himself bore our sins in his body on the tree, that we might die to sin and live to righteousness' (1 Pet. 2:24). After John Newton's spiritual birth, his speech immediately was set free from the profane oaths and blasphemies that previously filled it, never to be uttered again.[4]

2. **Routine maintenance.** Once the crop begins to grow, weeds keep emerging among the seedlings. The farmer can use a hoe or a mechanical plow to cut the roots of the weeds between the furrows. This controls the weeds, and allows the crop to prevail in the competition for moisture and nutrients. The key, however, is to catch the weeds early. Pull the weeds when they are small. Otherwise, their root system becomes entangled with the good plant, and they are much

---

4. Aitken, *John Newton: From Disgrace to Amazing Grace,* p. 94.

harder to destroy. 'For the grace of God has appeared ... training us to renounce ungodliness and worldly passions, and to live self-controlled, upright, and godly lives in the present age' (Titus 2:11).

3. **Outgrow the weeds.** If the good plants get an early jump on the weeds, the crop often will outgrow the weeds and eventually overwhelm them. This works particularly well with certain crops, such as wheat and oats. The same principle applies in the spiritual life of the believer. 'Put on then, as God's chosen ones, holy and beloved, compassionate hearts, kindness, humility, meekness, and patience, bearing with one another' (Col. 3:12-13). As grace grows, sin has less and less power. 'For sin will have no dominion over you, since you are not under law but under grace' (Rom. 6:14).

4. **Tolerate the weeds.** This may be the farmer's most interesting strategy. Though ideally there would not be a single weed in the field, the practical farmer knows that the final harvest will sort out the good from the bad. Jesus taught His followers in the parable of the weeds that 'the kingdom of heaven may be compared to a man who sowed good seed in his field, but while his men were sleeping, his enemy came and sowed weeds among the wheat and went away.' When the workers asked the master if they should uproot the weeds, he replied, 'No, lest in gathering the weeds you root up the wheat along with them. Let both grow together until the harvest, and at the harvest time I will tell the reapers, Gather the weeds first and bind them in bundles to be burned, but gather the wheat into my barn' (Matt. 13:24, 29-30). Spend more energy focusing on growing the good crop than fretting over the weeds that linger. We must be careful not to become complacent about tolerating known sin in our lives. But there is a

healthy balance in God's grace. We should carefully hear what Christ says to His followers. 'Bear fruit with patience' (Luke 8:15).

Knowing we face a lifelong battle, patience with ourselves and others is required. John Newton expressed this eloquently:

> Though sin wars, it shall not reign; and though it breaks our peace, it cannot separate us from his love. Nor is it inconsistent with his holiness and perfection, to manifest his favor to such poor defiled creatures, or to admit them to communion with himself; for they are not considered as themselves, but as one with Jesus, to whom they have fled for refuge, and by whom they live a life of faith. They are accepted in the Beloved, they have an Advocate with the Father, who once made an atonement for their sins, and ever lives to make intercession for their persons …There is a difference in kind between the feeblest efforts of faith in a real believer, while he is covered with shame at the thoughts of his miscarriages, and the highest and most specious attainments of those who are wise in their own eyes, and prudent in their own sight.

[5]The struggle to follow Christ is the very means He uses to transform us. Our recurring failure is met graciously and patiently with complete and utter forgiveness. While the consequences of our sin may linger, the penalty is gone. Bring your every sin, your every flaw, your every mistake of word or thought directly to Him, and you will be surprised by His grace. He is gentle and lowly, always quick to forgive and embrace.

Only by degrees and with setbacks are we weaned from relying on our own strength, our own wisdom, or our own resources, in the war against sin. Once we fully learn by experience the truth of Christ's words, 'Without me, you can

---

5. *Select Letters of John Newton*, pp. 150-151.

do nothing' (John 15:5) then, and only then, does transforming grace begin to mature.

A grace-filled sinner is not a person who no longer sins. There is no such thing. Rather, a grace-filled sinner is a child of God who has been embarrassed, frustrated, broken, harassed, and destroyed by his own sin, and therefore hungers and thirsts for righteousness.

Grace destroys the weeds.

6

THE PRUNING

'Every branch that does bear fruit he prunes, that it may bear more fruit' (John 15:2).

The comforting hymn, 'Whate're My God Ordains is Right,' was written by a seventeenth-century German pastor, Samuel Rodigast. He penned the lines as an encouragement for a friend and composer, Severus Gastorius, who was sick. Gastorius wrote a tune for the hymn, and it was published in the relatively obscure Weimar hymnal.

But the hymn reached its height of exposure when the great composer, Johann Sebastian Bach, discovered it in Leipzig, Germany, where he served as the court musician. Bach loved it, and wove the tune into several organ pieces and cantatas. The congregation sang it regularly in worship services at St. Thomas Church, where he was choral director.

Bach loved the hymn deeply, because he suffered deeply. Bach had lost both of his parents by age ten, and was raised by older siblings. Over the course of two marriages, he fathered twenty children of his own, many of whom died at birth. His first wife, Maria, who bore seven of the children, died suddenly at age 35. His second wife, Anna, bore him thirteen children. He was jailed at one point for several weeks when he angered Duke Wilhelm by requesting release from his position as court musician. The great composer later suffered blindness, failed eye surgeries, and ultimately died of a stroke at age 65. Along the way, there were economic hardships and political tensions among the states in Germany. Life was tough![1]

Painful trials cause us either to run toward God or run from God. How does His amazing grace factor into the dangers, toils, and snares of this life? Very directly – for our good and for His glory!

In the horticultural world, pruning is used on many different kinds of plants. Arborists and vintners selectively cut away weak, unhealthy, or crowded branches, which may become entry points for disease or insects, or simply rob vitality from the strongest branches. Vegetable growers may plant multiple seeds in a row or mound, then pull the smallest, least vibrant plants after they emerge, so the stronger ones can grow without competition. A wildlife manager mows a field of aging grass or clover, to 'refresh' the crop and promote new growth. Trimming, culling, thinning – these are all common methods of addition by subtraction. Pruning promotes new growth, opens the plant for penetration of sunlight and circulation of air, and concentrates the plant's energy into producing flowers or fruit. Simply put, pruning maximizes production.

The Lord does the same thing in the lives of His beloved children.

---

1. Radio Series: Hymns of the Faith, by Ligon Duncan, Derek Thomas, and Bill Wymond, Jan. 6, 2008, www.fpcjackson.org

WHAT IS SPIRITUAL PRUNING?

Some of the trials we experience, of course, we bring upon ourselves. Operating on the strength of our own self-dependence and self-righteousness, we fall headlong into all kinds of temptations and conflicts.

The Lord sometimes allows Satan to buffet His people, for His own glory. Listen to John Newton:

> [Satan] hates the Lord's people, grudges them all their privileges and all their comforts; and will do what he can to disquiet them, because he cannot prevail against them. And though the Lord sets such bounds to his rage as he cannot pass, and limits him both as to manner and time, he is often pleased to suffer him to discover his malice to a considerable degree; not to gratify Satan, but to humble and prove *them* …. Though temptations, in their own nature, are grievous and dreadful, yet when, by the grace of God, they are productive of these effects, they deserve to be numbered among the 'all things which are appointed to work together for the good of those who love him.'[2]

Whatever the root cause, it is clear in Scripture that the Lord uses the trials in our lives to stimulate us and produce more fruit. Thus, we are warned that suffering of various kinds is to be expected: 'do not be surprised at the fiery trial when it comes upon you to test you, as though something strange were happening to you' (1 Pet. 4:12). In fact, suffering is actually one of the Lord's best tools for growing us in grace. The Lord tests every believer to strengthen and confirm them, and chastises every wayward son or daughter, to correct and refine them.

Often, believers run into conflict with the world because they publicly identify themselves with Christ, whom the world

---

2. *Select Letters of John Newton*, p. 103.

rejects. 'All who desire to live a godly life in Christ Jesus will be persecuted' (2 Tim. 3:12). The world hates our Master, therefore the world hates us (John 15:19). Yet grace turns their curse into a blessing. He sovereignly superintends their hatred, using trials to wean His children from the love of this world, to strengthen their faith, and to produce in them a deep luster of grace that otherwise would never emerge. The very weapons that are fashioned against us will only accelerate the growth of grace in our lives. 'Affliction,' said Martin Luther, 'is the best book in my library.'[3]

THE BENEFITS OF PRUNING

The benefits of pruning trees and plants are profound. The remaining branches are healthier and produce more fruit. Christ does the same with all His followers. 'Every branch in me that does not bear fruit he takes away, and every branch that does bear fruit he prunes, that it may bear more fruit' (John 15:2). Suffering comes in many packages, but has rich spiritual benefits:

1. Focuses our thinking. 'Since therefore Christ suffered in the flesh, arm yourselves with the same way of thinking, for whoever has suffered in the flesh has ceased from sin, so as to live for the rest of the time in the flesh no longer for human passions but for the will of God' (1 Pet. 4:1-2). The expression 'has ceased from sin' does not mean 'never sins at all.' That would be contrary to other passages in Scripture, which clearly state that we will never be entirely free from sin in this life (e.g., James 3:2, and 1 John 1:8). Rather,

---

3. David B. Calhoun, *In Their Own Words,* The Banner of Truth Trust, 2018, p. 50.

it means 'has made a clear break with sin,'[4] to the point that obeying God, rather than avoiding hardship, is the believer's primary motivation in life. At one level, anyone who has walked with a loved one through a long illness, or has experienced a great loss, sees more clearly the things that really matter in life. We have all heard cancer or accident victims say, 'It was the best thing that ever happened to me. It changed me forever.' The same focus comes to the one who suffers persecution or abuse on account of their faith. There is a seriousness and a spiritual growth that comes by God's grace. Suffering makes us more sober-minded, and focuses our attention on relationships and the priorities that matter most in life.

Johann Sebastian Bach, as mentioned, suffered many trials and losses in life, but, rather than dimming his faith, they deepened it. His life and work were entirely committed to his Savior, most significantly his music. At the end of each musical score he composed, Bach habitually penciled the letters, 'I.N.J.', abbreviating the Latin phrase, 'in nomine Jesu' ('in the name of Jesus').

2. <u>Filters our passions</u>. 'For the time that is past suffices for doing what the Gentiles want to do, living in sensuality, passions, drunkenness, orgies, drinking parties, and lawless idolatry' (1 Pet. 4:3). Let's be honest: wild living is exhausting. What is worse, it also gets pretty boring, unless we keep supersizing it to get a bigger thrill. Ironically, pleasure from sin is subject to the law of diminishing returns. It takes bigger, wilder experiences to create the same excitement. (That is why sexual promiscuity leads inevitably to isolation, frustration, and brokenness, while marital fidelity is endlessly fresh and satisfying. See Proverbs 5 for vivid

---

4. Wayne Grudem, *1 Peter*, Tyndale New Testament Commentaries, Inter-Varsity Press, 1995, p. 167.

details.) When God graciously intervenes, our self-inflicted or God-appointed aches, pains, and struggles in life have a way of sobering us up, allowing us to see the foolishness of living for our passions. Sin gets stale, but grace is endlessly fresh. And fresh grace brings a new level of self-control.

3. <u>Fits us for heaven</u>. God's main agenda for our life is *not* that we will be perpetually healthy, wealthy, and stress-free, but that we will grow in grace. 'For this is why the gospel was preached ... that though judged in the flesh the way people are, they might live in the spirit the way God does' (1 Pet. 4:6). We know that, though our physical body will fade away, our soul will live forever. A prime by-product of suffering in the flesh, therefore, is to prepare us for heaven: 'This light momentary affliction is preparing for us an eternal weight of glory beyond all comparison' (2 Cor. 4:17).

Any farmer or rancher knows that the grasses sheep and cattle like to eat have a 'growth point' at or near the ground. When the animal bites off a blade of grass or a stem of clover, for example, the plant quickly regrows from this growth point. The cutting actually stimulates the plant to grow faster and stronger. So it is with our suffering, by God's grace.

4. <u>Forms good fruit</u>. The natural man, apart from grace, produces only thorns and wild grapes. Though he may display the common graces of civility and integrity at one level, these are merely outward manifestations of a self-centered life. John Owen, the seventeenth-century pastor, said,

> The heart is like the sluggard's field, so overgrown with weeds that you can scarce see the good corn ... But let the heart be cleansed by mortification, and the

weeds of lust constantly and daily rooted up (as they spring daily, nature being their proper soil), there will be room for grace to thrive and flourish, the graces that God gives will act their part, and be ready for every use and purpose![5]

Christlikeness emerges only as true grace produces its fruit in us, the chief attribute of which is love. As we will see in the next chapter, the God-given, self-sacrificing love (agape) imparted to the believer 'as good stewards of the manifold grace of God' (1 Pet. 4:10 NASB) focuses no longer on self. The growing believer produces the sweet fruit of genuine affection toward God and others.

5. Forges in us Christ's glory. Ric Furrer is a blacksmith in Sturgeon Bay, Wisconsin, who specializes in the slow and difficult art of hand-forging swords and other ancient weapons. Each one is painstakingly crafted:

> What may take me 100 blows by hand can be accomplished in one by a large swaging machine. This is the antithesis of my goal and to that end all my work shows evidence of the two hands that made it.[6]

As a skilled blacksmith heats an ingot of steel in a hot furnace, then places the softened metal on the anvil and strikes it repeatedly with a hammer to shape it, so the Lord uses the trials and tribulations of life to fashion us into the image of Christ. 'Beloved, do not be surprised at the fiery trial when it comes upon you to test you, as though something strange were happening to you. But rejoice insofar as you share Christ's sufferings, that you may also rejoice and

5. John Owen, *The Mortification of Sin,* The Banner of Truth Trust, 2004, p. 25.

6. Cal Newport, *Deep Work,* Grand Central Publishing, 2016, p. 72.

be glad when his glory is revealed' (1 Pet. 4: 12-13). The pattern of Christ's glorification through His suffering is repeated on a smaller scale in the lives of His children, 'for to this you have been called, because Christ also suffered for you' (1 Pet. 2:21).

As we look to Jesus and ask Him to walk with us in our trials, His all-sufficient grace is infused more and more deeply into our souls. A profound transformation begins to take place, which Paul called 'Christ in you, the hope of glory' (Col. 1:27). The outcome is maturity in Christ, as His Spirit powerfully works within us.

The child of God, knowing His best interests are safe, is not greatly afraid of evil, but enjoys a stable place in an unstable world. Only pruning can produce such a result.

DESPAIR MEETS GRACE

An irony of the Christian life is that God often walks with us most closely in times of suffering. The Lord pours out a special measure of peace (Phil. 4:7), contentment (Phil. 4:11), and strength (Phil. 4:13), when we actively trust His gracious and wise ways in the midst of our despair. 'Therefore let those who suffer according to God's will entrust their souls to a faithful Creator while doing good' (1 Pet. 4:19).

In fact, grace abounds in times of suffering. By grace, the Lord upholds the believer, assuring him 'that chastisements are a token of his love; that the season, measure, and continuance of his sufferings are appointed by infinite wisdom, and designed to work for his everlasting good; and that grace and strength will be afforded him, according to his day.'[7]

---

7. *Select Letters of John Newton,* p. 93.

Dr. Dale Ralph Davis, a former pastor at First Presbyterian Church in Columbia, South Carolina, said in a sermon that King David learned this lesson early in life, and it served him to the end. In 1 Samuel 26, we find King Saul jealously pursuing the young warrior, David, in the wilderness, to kill him. One night, surrounded by an encampment of 3,000 soldiers, Saul and the whole camp fell into a deep sleep. David was able to slip into his enemy's camp and retrieve the king's spear, which was stuck in the ground by his head, and his water jar, then retreat from the camp without harming the king. The next morning, David stood outside their camp and held up his trophies, to demonstrate that he had walked in their midst and had passed up the opportunity to kill his persecutor. David demonstrated in this incident two key principles for walking faithfully in times of suffering or persecution. First, he refused to take a short cut to bring this trial to an end. He had a kind of faith that sticks to the path of obedience. David knew that God forbids murder, and David was properly constrained by his conscience from taking revenge against Saul when he had the opportunity. Saul was the Lord's anointed king of Israel at the time, and David would leave it to the Lord to end his difficult trial. Often, we know how we should behave, and where our duty lies (e.g., marital faithfulness, parental discipline, job integrity), but we desperately want out of the trouble in which we find ourselves. We are always called to walk faithfully in the Lord's ways, though we do not know how or when the Lord will resolve our pain. Suffering is not a license to take short-cuts.

Secondly, we see that David had the kind of faith that finds 'tokens' of God's encouragement in the middle of our trials. Saul's captured water jar (a symbol of life-giving water in the wilderness) and the spear (a symbol of the king's power) were signs to David of God's sovereign provision and favor. 'David got the point,' said Davis. Faith looks for, and finds, encouragement in God's covenant provisions to His children. Sometimes these gifts are dramatic, but more often they are subtle and quiet. A word of encouragement from a friend; a touch on the hand from someone who knows our pain; a good word in a passage of Scripture. The Lord's gifts come with the Lord's afflictions, no matter how small. Grace looks for those encouragements, remembers them, and thanks God for them.

Being thankful for what God has given, rather than resentful for what He has withheld, is the fruit of mature faith.

SUFFERING IS ONLY FOR A SEASON

'The Lord knows how to rescue the godly from trials' (2 Pet. 2:9). And, in the meantime, He knows how to sustain and refine His people in and through life's burdens. Few understood this better than Thomas Boston, a Puritan pastor in Ettrick, in southern Scotland. Boston suffered for years from theological battles within the Church of Scotland, his wife's paralyzing depression, and, for the last eight years of his life, from his own recurring bouts with kidney stones. These stresses together left him a physical wreck. In Boston's autobiography, he called these years 'the groaning part of my life.'

Yet before Boston died in 1732 at the age of fifty-six, he began writing a book on the lessons he had learned, expounding a text from Ecclesiastes 7:13, 'Consider the work of God; who can make straight what he has made crooked?' The nearly-completed treatise was entitled: 'The Crook in the Lot: The Sovereignty and Wisdom of God in the Afflictions of Men Displayed.' After his death, friends completed and published his book in 1737, which is a goldmine of insight into the doctrine of true grace in times of suffering.

As Boston explains, the 'crook' is the twisted or difficult thing in our lives, such as illness, grief, or any kind of pain or loss. The 'lot' is our circumstances, the condition in which we find ourselves when the suffering occurs. The point of the text is that God alone can remove the difficulty from us, and teach us that we can trust Him, even when the bottom falls out. In such times, the Christian believer is exhorted to:

1. *Pray for the crook's removal.* 'Is anyone among you suffering? Let him pray' (James 5:13). As we suffer anxieties and cares, our heavenly Father invites us to draw near to Him, and unload our burdens at the throne of grace.

2. *Humble yourself under the trial.* Consider whether you have contributed in some way to the situation which now vexes you. David, the psalmist, developed a habit of self-examination. 'Search me, O God, and know my heart! Try me and know my thoughts! And see if there is any grievous way in me, and lead me in the way everlasting!' (Ps. 139:23-24). Ask God to show you how you may have fallen short, and give you strength and grace to lean on Him for help.

3. *Confess sin.* As the Lord brings our faults and mistakes into focus, be quick to confess the harsh words, sinful attitudes, and back-biting actions you have launched against others, and any resentment with the Lord Himself. Once David saw his own wickedness, he pled guilty and asked for restoration: 'Blot out all my iniquities. Create in me a clean heart, O God, and renew a right spirit within me' (Ps. 51:9-10). The Lord is faithful and just to forgive, and to cleanse us from all unrighteousness. His compassion toward us is great, because He knows our frame, He is mindful that we are but dust (Ps. 103:14).

4. *Confessing sin is difficult,* but the writer of Hebrews says the pain of correction is our loving Father's way with His children: 'For the moment, all discipline seems painful

rather than pleasant, but later it yields the peaceful fruit of righteousness to those who have been trained by it' (Heb. 12:11). The tendrils of grace train us, bending us toward God's ways. The reshaping can hurt, but it yields great fruit when we say, 'I was wrong. Please forgive me.' It gives us peace when we retrace our steps, acknowledge where we left the path, and return to a right relationship with God and others.

5. *Wait patiently.* Waiting patiently does not mean waiting passively. Though it sounds contradictory, Christian waiting is an active form of resting, in which we watch, pray, trust, and think, knowing that God is sovereign, He is good, and He is working out His purposes in our lives. As He sanctifies even our deepest distress, He changes us and refines us. As Dr. Glen Knecht, a former pastor at First Presbyterian Church in Columbia, often said, we should 'levy a tax' on our suffering, extracting benefit from the burden.

6. *Express the pain.* The book of Lamentations teaches us a valuable principle about suffering. Probably written by the prophet Jeremiah, who suffered greatly, Lamentations is written in a highly structured style. Four of the five chapters (one, two, four and five) are each 22 verses long, and each verse begins with a sequential letter of the Hebrew alphabet. The third chapter of the book (the mid-point, as is common in Hebrew literature, for emphasis) is 66 verses long, being written in a 'triple' acrostic style. This intentional format gives 'full expression' to the lament, as the writer patiently re-examines and thoughtfully expresses the pain of Israel's affliction, searching for words that coherently express his grief.

The central passage of Lamentations contains this profound promise:

> The steadfast love of the LORD never ceases, his mercies never come to an end; they are new every morning; great is your faithfulness. 'The LORD is my portion,' says my soul, 'therefore I will hope in him.' The LORD is good to those who wait for him, to the soul who seeks him … For the Lord will not cast off forever, but though he cause grief, he will have compassion according to the abundance of his steadfast love (Lam. 3:22-25, 31-32).

When we experience a great loss or deep suffering, we generally want to just put it behind us and forget it. But Scripture teaches us to carefully take stock of what the Lord may be doing. Deep mourning is worth our best effort, as we give intellectual, emotional, and even artistic expression to our grief.

1. *Go to the sanctuary.* Yahweh's presence can be found in public worship, and this is especially comforting in times of distress or when tempted to compare ourselves to others, who seem to have an easy life. The psalmist discovered a new sense of God's greatness in the sanctuary:

> Behold, these are the wicked; and always at ease, they have increased in wealth. Surely in vain I have kept my heart pure, and washed my hands in innocence; for I have been stricken all day long, and chastened every morning … When I pondered to understand this, it was troublesome in my sight until I came into the sanctuary of God, then I perceived their end (Ps. 73:12-14, 16-17).

Today's trials come into focus when we worship.

2. *Treasure the sacraments.* The sacraments are a sign and seal of the Lord's blessing. As we reflect on baptism, we see afresh the 'acted parable' of the washing away of our sins,

and know that the Lord loves us supremely. As we celebrate the Lord's supper, the meaning of the communion bread and the wine are powerful reminders: as bread nourishes the body and wine refreshes the soul, so the Lord promises always to strengthen and sustain us.

3. *Reach out to Christ for an exchange.* Thomas Boston learned a valuable lesson:

> There is never a crook which God makes in our lot, but it is in effect heaven's offer of a blessed exchange to us .... God first puts out his hand, and takes away some earthly thing from us, and it is expected we put out our hand next, and take some heavenly thing from him in the stead of it .... Therefore the soul's closing with Christ is called buying, wherein parting with one thing, we get another in its stead.[8]

That is why James says, 'Consider it all joy, my brethren, when you encounter various trials, knowing that the testing of your faith produces endurance' (James 1:2 NASB). When we reach the point where we accept the loss and trust the Father for His promise to cause all things – even *this* thing – to work together for our good, we have advanced in the work of grace.

SUFFERING MAKES OR BREAKS

At the end of the day, pruning has a profound impact on spiritual growth, for better or worse. For some, trials bring them quickly to a terminal point in the walk of faith. They are the ones who 'in time of testing fall away' (Luke 8:13). Others emerge from trials closer to God and filled with more grace. Peter exhorts us to press on with Christ: 'the tested genuineness

---

8. *The Crook in the Lot,* p. 65.

of your faith – more precious than gold that perishes though it is tested by fire – may be found to result in praise and glory and honor at the revelation of Jesus Christ' (1 Pet. 1: 6-7). Pruning causes the plant to respond by putting down deeper roots and producing new growth. Praise God, the master gardener, for His gracious ways.

What is the new growth that emerges from pruning? Solid joy! 'We rejoice in our sufferings, knowing that suffering produces endurance, and endurance produces character, and character produces hope' (Rom. 5:3-4). Suffering builds our *endurance*, refines our *character*, and brightens our *hope*. John Newton's robust hymn, *Glorious Things of Thee Are Spoken*, reminds us: 'fading is the worldling's pleasure, all his boasted pomp and show; solid joys and lasting treasure none but Zion's children know.'

Will you trust God for grace in times of pruning? Ask Him for strength, by the power of His glorious grace, to give you endurance and patience. Knowing that He uses trials to stimulate new spiritual growth, lean into Him for His all-sufficiency. Ask Him to refine away the dross, leaving more of Himself and less of your self-sufficiency in the cup. Look for Jesus in every challenge, setback, and disappointment. Ask for the grace of contentment in all circumstances. He gives rest to the weary.

Grace prunes the branches.

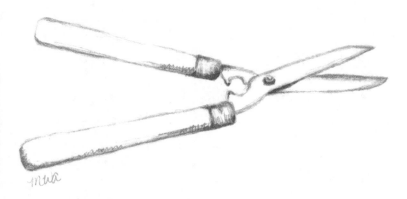

7

THE FRUIT

'The fruit of the Spirit is love, joy, peace, patience,
kindness, goodness, faithfulness, gentleness, self-control'
(Gal. 5:22-23).

'Give me books, French wine, fruit, fine weather, and a little music played out of doors,' said John Keats, the English Romantic poet.

But how can you be sure if a Merlot or Cabernet Sauvignon at the local market is authentic French wine, not a cheap imitation? Counterfeits abound, but the best wine takes on the unique qualities of the soil and climate of its region – expressing the 'soul' of the grapes. So in the early 1900s, the French government established the IOC, its official 'Institut de l'Origine et de la Qualité.' The IOC rigorously tests and monitors vineyards throughout the grape growing and winemaking process, awarding only the best wines of a region the coveted designation as 'appellation d'origine contrôlée'

(AOC). The AOC stamp is a guarantee of both authenticity and quality.

How does one know if a follower of Jesus Christ is a genuine disciple? Jesus said, 'Every healthy tree bears good fruit … Thus, you will recognize them by their fruits' (Matt. 7:17, 20). A good vine in good soil produces good fruit. So believers take on the spiritual characteristics of the root stock from which they are grown. The grace of Jesus imparts a rich, distinctive flavor to souls who cling to Him, which others can discern.

All good fruit is (i) powered by the Spirit, (ii) producing in us Christlikeness, and (iii) pleasing to the Father. Notice the Trinity, as Father, Son and Spirit conspire together to work out their gardening plan.

POWERED BY THE SPIRIT

I first ventured sailing in a small, single-masted craft called a Sunfish, ironically named the 'Miss Joy.' I was new to Charleston at the time, and the romantic notion of a breezy harbor tour seemed appealing. I was so naïve. No sooner had I pushed off from the dock than the chaotic, turbulent forces of the wind, the waves, and the wake from a passing shrimp boat nearly capsized me. But my greatest miscalculation was the power of the tide. The moment I pushed my small craft away from the dock, the outgoing tide grabbed it and pulled me swiftly toward the shipping channel, where real danger awaited. Panicked, I struggled to hoist the sail. When I finally hauled the sheet to the top of the mast, wind filled the sail, and the boat quickly came about in the right direction. The wind easily overruled the pull of the tide, and I was free to navigate toward safety.

Sin's grip on us is like the tide: our natural thoughts, feelings and appetites pull us along life's path. But once the Spirit enters our life, His influence is greater than the pull of sin. In his letter to the Galatians, Paul describes our freedom in Christ, when, by faith, we are set free from the dominion of sin. He reminds us that the Spirit is given to empower us to freely serve the Lord and others, not just ourselves: 'You were called to freedom, brothers. Only do not use your freedom as an opportunity for the flesh, but through love serve one another' (Gal. 5:13). True liberty is not freedom to live as we want, but freedom to express the very potential for which we were created: enjoying a restored relationship with Him and loving and serving others. Only if we 'walk by the Spirit' (Gal. 5:16, 25) and are 'led by the Spirit' (Gal. 5:18) can we develop such fruit of the Spirit. The word for 'Spirit' in Greek is *pneuma,* which literally means 'breath' or 'wind'. To be led by the Spirit means to be carried along in life, animated by the power of the Spirit.

The most impressive demonstration of wind power I have personally witnessed was when Hurricane Hugo made landfall in Charleston in September 1989. The eye of the Category 4 storm passed directly over the historic city, with devastating, 100-mile per hour sustained winds. The storm surge pushed ashore by the hurricane-force winds flooded much of the low-lying coastal area with more than fifteen feet of water. Massive trees were toppled, large yachts and trawlers were carried inland, and metal roofs were peeled from homes like paper in the wind.

With that picture in mind, hear the words of Paul: 'I pray that you may know what is the immeasurable greatness of his power toward us who believe, according to the working of his great might' (Eph. 1:19). Applied to our daily lives, if we walk by the Spirit we will not gratify (be pulled along by) the desires of the flesh. Those who belong to Christ can overcome the power of the flesh with its passions and desires. This transformation comes in fits and starts, to be sure, with frequent setbacks and reversals. But the dominating power of the Spirit *will* carry us forward. Every branch that abides in Christ *will* bear fruit.

John Newton wrote to a friend about the practical influence of faith on the believer:

> The faith which justifies the soul does likewise receive from Jesus grace for grace, whereby the heart is purified, and the conversation regulated as becomes the Gospel of Christ ... We have the authority and example of St. Paul, who was a champion of the doctrines of free grace, to animate us in exhorting believers to 'walk worthy of God, who has called them to his kingdom and glory'... It is a believer's privilege to walk with God in the exercise of faith, and by the power of his Spirit, to mortify the body of sin; to gain a growing victory over the world and self, and to make advances in conformity to the mind that was in Christ.[1]

Growing in grace is not a self-help project. We cannot make ourselves more loving, kind, and gentle by the power of positive thinking. Deep transformation and true grace come only when the Spirit draws us into a daily walk with Jesus. Paul underscores the vital connection with Jesus: 'Through him we have obtained access by faith into this grace in which we stand' (Rom. 5:2).

PRODUCING CHRISTLIKENESS

Notice an interesting aspect of Paul's text in Galatians 5. He describes the 'works of the flesh' in the plural, whereas he describes the 'fruit of the Spirit' in the singular, as a collective noun. Works versus fruit. The works of sin are disjointed and incoherent, just as our words and actions are often inconsistent with our inner desires and objectives. But the fruit of the

---

1. *Select Letters of John Newton*, p. 91.

Spirit is integrated and logical. When we are attached to Jesus – absorbing His words, resting in His love, talking to Him regularly through prayer – we experience that life-transforming, life-integrating connection. Such a personal relationship with our Savior slowly but naturally wears off on us. Think of the influence of grace flowing from Jesus like a lifeline or like the sap that begins to move in the vines each Spring.

I think that's what John meant when he said, 'And the Word became flesh and dwelt among us, ... and from his fullness we have all received, grace upon grace' (John 1:14, 16). If we are connected to Jesus, the gracious effect of His life on ours is irrepressible. We are recipients of His grace, and become instruments of His grace toward others. Scripture calls this change our 'sanctification,' as we become more like Jesus. You can't stop it from happening, if you abide in Christ. 'I chose you and appointed you that you should go and bear fruit and that your fruit should abide' (John 15:16).

What 'fruit' does Christ cause us to bear? Paul gave the Galatians a sampler of the fruit. My wife Cathy loves chocolate, so I occasionally buy her a chocolate sampler. Chocolate makers select a few of their most popular (or maybe their least popular!) products, and sell them in an assortment. Opening the box, you first savor that wonderful smell. Then you try to sort out which ones are fruit-filled, which ones are nut-filled, and, best of all, which ones are pure, rich chocolate. Usually, there is a guide inside the box, identifying the candies by their different shapes and colors.

Paul's list is a sampler of the fruit the Holy Spirit is producing in Christ's people. He says, 'The fruit of the Spirit is love, joy, peace, patience, kindness, goodness, faithfulness, gentleness, self-control' (Gal. 5:22-23). The list is not exhaustive. Other characteristics such as humility, thankfulness, contentment, and generosity, to name a few, could have easily been included.

It's a sampler, not a complete inventory of the change grace manifests in us. Grace is such a multi-faceted jewel that it cannot be fully described in nine words.

Let's look more closely at the characteristics being formed in us by the Spirit:

- Love ('agape') – God-given, supreme affection for Himself and others, derived from the essential nature of God. God is love. This divine love is self-sacrificing, to the point of death, for the well-being of others.

- Joy ('chara') – gladness; delighted contentment in all circumstances, knowing that God works all things together for my good and His glory.

- Peace ('eirene') – rest; quietness; harmony with God first, and therefore with myself and others. Sinclair Ferguson says, 'Peace is joy resting; joy is peace dancing.'

- Patience ('makrothumia') – forbearance; longsuffering; waiting for God to act or intervene.

- Kindness ('chrestotes') – affection or warmth genuinely felt and expressed toward others; the twin sibling of goodness.

- Goodness ('agathosune') – grace in action; kindness expressed in selfless and tangible ways; generously sharing one's time, reputation, or resources with others, for their good, not for personal gain.

- Faithfulness ('pistis') – fidelity; constancy; unfailing reliability, like the Marine Corps motto, 'Semper Fidelis.'

- Gentleness ('prautes') – not disputing or demanding, based on reliance toward God; power under control; the opposite of self-assertive. The gentle person is safe to approach, and unfailingly helpful.

- Self-control ('enkrateia') – disciplined and moderate in one's thoughts, words, and actions; the controlling power of the will over passions and temptations, by the influence of the Spirit.

Notice several things about the fruit. First, it is the fruit *of the Spirit*. It is not the outgrowth of our natural personality or disposition. Nor is it the fruit of good education or training, which may produce polite citizens who have learned to play well with others, but who do so principally for their own benefit or self-approval. Nor is it the product of futile self-help efforts to reform our thoughts, words and deeds. We are dead in our trespasses, slaves to sin, and unable to reform ourselves, apart from God's grace! Only through the lifeline of the Holy Spirit will true fruit emerge.

Second, notice that the list begins with the most important quality first: *love*. In every prioritized list, like this one, love is first. In every ascending list, love is the pinnacle. For example, in his letter to the Colossians, Paul capped off a list of graces with the greatest: 'Put on then ... compassionate hearts, kindness, humility, meekness and patience ... And above all these put on love' (Col. 3:12, 14). But a true love of God and others is exactly what we lack. Love is the fountain source, the essential, first quality, from which the other attributes spring, and in which the others are rooted. Love is the glue which binds all of the others together in perfect balance and harmony (Col. 3:14). Love is the essential grace without which all the other qualities are nothing (1 Cor. 13:1-3). This kind of love only comes from Christ's Spirit dwelling in us. 'God's love has been poured into our hearts through the Holy Spirit who has been given to us' (Rom. 5:5). Such love, if it is in us, colors how we view and treat others. 'Love one another as I have loved you' (John 15:12). By grace, we become imitators of God, walking in love. But only by abiding in His love do we have true love to share with others.

Third, notice that the fruit, like grapes, is *collective*. It grows in clusters: three groupings of three characteristics each that are directed Godward, man-ward, and self-ward. The first cluster (love, joy and peace) characterizes our relationship with God. Remember Jesus's teaching that the first and great commandment is to love God with all your heart and with all your soul and with all your mind (Matt. 22:37-38). This triad is the foundation of what follows. The next cluster (patience, kindness, and goodness) summarizes our relationship with others. Again, Christ said the second great commandment is that we love our neighbor as we love ourselves (Matt. 22:39). The last cluster describes the believer's relationship with himself, that is, the basic tone of his inner life. Faithfulness, gentleness, and self-control become the core of our inner narrative, when grace is having its effect in us. These three clusters of divine fruit hang together:

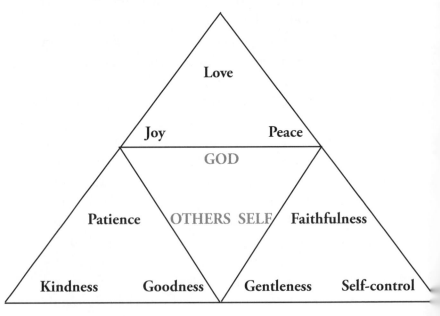

Fourth, notice that the fruit is *quiet*, not brash or self-promoting. Grace does not blow a trumpet to draw attention to itself. Jesus grew up the son of a humble carpenter, and worked with His hands. When He began His public ministry, He never mounted a promotional campaign or deployed strategies to highlight His miraculous gifts. In fact, He often instructed the beneficiaries of His healing powers to tell no one who had healed them! Paul instructed the believers in Thessalonica to 'aspire to live quietly' (1 Thess. 4:11) and to 'do their work quietly' (2 Thess. 3:12). He reminded Timothy to pray specifically 'that we may lead a peaceful and quiet life in all godliness' (1 Tim. 2:2). Jesus, who alone developed and displayed the fruit of the Spirit perfectly, said, 'Take my yoke upon you, and learn from me, for I am gentle and lowly in heart' (Matt. 11:29). Gentle, quiet lives are the sweet fruit of grace.

Fifth, notice that grace is *calm* and unruffled. Jesus was never in a hurry or frustrated, never caught up in urgency. When news came that His beloved friend Lazarus was near death, He waited two days to go to him (John 11:6). When His disciples implored Him to leave His prayer retreat on the mountain to heal the many sick among the restless crowd, He demurred. 'Let us go on to the next towns, that I may preach there also, for that is why I came' (Mark 1:38). Jesus often withdrew alone to a garden or mountain top to pray to His Father, 'as was his custom' (Luke 22:39). Filled with the Spirit, His perfect love and trust for the Father slowed Him down, and made Him certain to do the important things, not the urgent things. And that spilled over into how He served, ministered to, and taught others. To minister to others with grace, we, too, need to balance time 'in here' with service 'out there.' We must feed our own souls before trying to meet the needs of others.

Finally, notice there is a *consistency* or harmony between inner motives (what's inside our heart) and outer manifestations (how we treat others). What comes out of the fruit is what is inside the fruit: grace!

These godly attributes are not merely future aspirations for how we will live in heaven. The Spirit begins forming this fruit in us now, though gradually and imperfectly, to prove that our faith in Christ is genuine. Jesus taught His followers, 'Every healthy tree bears fruit ... you will recognize them by their fruits' (Matt. 7:17, 20).

So, what does grace look like in the believer's life, even while growing in poor, weed-infested soil? How does grace manifest itself in practical ways? Paul applied these fruits in Romans 12:1-21, when he instructed believers to love and serve others in the church 'according to the grace given to us':

Galatians 5: The Fruit	Romans 12: The Flavor
Love	Let love be genuine (v.9); love one another with brotherly affection (v.10).
Joy	Rejoice in hope (v.12).
Peace	Live in harmony with one another (v.16); live peaceably with all (v.18).
Patience	Be patient in tribulation (v.12).
Kindness	Contribute to the needs of the saints, and seek to show hospitality (v.13).
Goodness	Hold fast to what is good (v.9); overcome evil with good (v. 21).
Faithfulness	Do what is honorable in the sight of all (v.17).
Gentleness	Never avenge yourselves (v.19).
Self-control	Present your bodies as a living sacrifice, holy and acceptable to God (v.1).

With inward and outward changes, grace blossoms and bears fruit in the lives of God's children. Consider a beautiful case study of grace in full bloom. Aquila and Priscilla were an ordinary couple who did some extraordinary things for the kingdom. They 'risked their necks' to save the life of the Apostle Paul (Rom. 16:4). They hosted a church in their home (Rom. 16:5). They gently corrected the theology of a popular and gifted preacher, Apollos, 'and explained to him the way of God more accurately' (Acts 18:26). Their lives had the aroma of authentic grace.

The same could be said of the unnamed widows in 1 Timothy 5, who 'performed good works' by bringing up children in the faith (faithfulness in family life), showing hospitality (serving strangers), washing the feet of the saints (ministering to others in humble ways within the church), and caring for the afflicted (comforting others).

Grace makes us useful to others, but especially to those within the household of believers.

PLEASING TO THE FATHER

Swirl the glass, inhale the aroma, and taste the sweetness. Grace imparts a distinctive flavor to our lives, as every follower becomes a 'product of Christ.' This is the outworking, the living proof of the efficacy of the covenant of grace.

The person growing in grace pleases the Father, and all enmity with Him has been resolved. When Paul says of the fruit in Galatians 5:23, 'against such things there is no law,' he asserts there is no longer any penalty under the law because we have been redeemed. In a similar way, he says elsewhere:

> There is therefore now no condemnation for those who are in Christ Jesus. For the law of the Spirit of life has set you free in Christ Jesus from the law of sin and death. For God has done

what the law, weakened by the flesh, could not do … in order that the righteous requirement of the law might be fulfilled in us, who walk not according to the flesh but according to the Spirit (Rom. 8:1-4).

The power of God will accomplish the purposes of God: to create children who bear His image and reflect His character. In Isaiah's 'Song of the Vineyard,' the Lord Himself says, 'In that day, a pleasant vineyard, sing of it! I, the LORD, am its keeper; every moment I water it … I keep it night and day … In days to come Jacob will take root, Israel shall blossom and put forth shoots and fill the whole world with fruit' (Isa. 27:2-3, 6). Grace is the fruitful life of God, redeeming and transforming the soul of man.

Growing in grace is not merely a good thing – like getting enough exercise or flossing your teeth regularly. It is the primary goal in life! Jesus instructed His followers, 'By this my Father is glorified, that you bear much fruit and so prove to be my disciples' (John 15:8). Grace derived by the Spirit produces grace displayed toward others. 'For we are his workmanship, created in Christ Jesus for good works, which God prepared beforehand, that we should walk in them' (Eph. 2:10). Bearing fruit for God's glory and enjoying Him forever is our chief end. To be rich in grace is to be rich in good works, generous to others, and ready to share. In doing so, we 'take hold of that which is truly life' (1 Tim. 6:19). Grace is living with a singular focus on eternity.

When our granddaughter, Eliza Ann, was three, she wanted her own little broom and dust pan to help sweep the floors. Her desire to help far exceeded her ability to help. In fact, her efforts just moved the dirt around. But it warmed our hearts, and before long she began to get the hang of it. Skill comes with practice, and maturity with time.

So the transforming grace of growing obedience marks every believer. 'By this it is evident who are the children of God, and who are the children of the devil: whoever does not practice righteousness is not of God, nor is the one who does not love his brother' (1 John 3:10). As we walk with Christ, spending more and more time with Him, we begin to look and act more like Him. The relationship wears off on us, and His grace slowly transforms us. The general pattern of our life honors and pleases Christ, as we learn to know and trust Him better.

The feeling of progress may wax and wane. But the promise stands: He who began a good work in you will bring it to completion. He is not only the one who plants the seed of faith, but He is also the one who brings it to maturity. A sailor far offshore, watching the distant shoreline, sees no immediate sign of progress. But as the hours pass, the scenery quietly changes.

GIFTS OF GRACE

What does 'bearing fruit' look like? We may have the mistaken idea that grace is primarily a personal adornment, making us more attractive or acceptable to God. But it extends far beyond that. Grace is given to effect change in others as well. Grace employs us as co-laborers with God. Paul describes it this way: 'Grace was given to each one of us according to the measure of Christ's gift ... he gave the apostles, the prophets, the evangelists, the shepherds, and teachers, to equip the saints for the work of ministry, for building up the body of Christ, until we all attain to the unity of the faith and of the knowledge of the Son of God, to mature manhood' (Eph. 4:7-13). These 'gifts of grace' fall into two broad categories: the 'speaking' gifts (such as pastors, teachers, encouragers, etc.), which enable us to speak words of life to others, and the 'service' gifts (such as helping others, organizing, giving, etc.), which enable us to lead or serve others in tangible ways. See the passages in Romans 12 and 1 Corinthians 12 (the 'twelves') and Ephesians 4 and 1 Peter 4 (the 'fours') for a deeper study of spiritual gifts.

The spiritual gifts are for the common good of the church, not for the praise or recognition of the servant who bears them. They are gifts, not something we selected or developed on our own, so there is no reason to boast. They are practical, intended to genuinely help others in both spiritual and material ways. James reminds us that being heavenly-minded expresses itself by doing earthly good: 'If a brother or sister is poorly clothed and lacking in daily food, and one of you says to them, "Go in peace, be warmed and filled," without giving them the things needed for the body, what good is that?' (James 2:15-16). Like manure, grace is of little value unless we spread it around!

The more humble gifts, humanly speaking, are actually the most honored and preferable gifts, and most precious in God's sight. It is not the person up front, who is seen by all, but the one who labors humbly and quietly behind the scenes, who earns the greatest praise from our Father. As Paul put it so graphically, 'If the foot should say, "Because I am not a hand, I do not belong to the body," that would not make it any less a part of the body … On the contrary, the parts of the body that seem to be weaker are indispensable, and on those parts of the body that we think less honorable, we bestow the greater honor' (1 Cor. 12:15, 22-23). Every part is essential for the well-being of the body. Therefore, 'be good stewards of God's varied grace' (1 Pet. 4:10), putting into practice whatever gift you have been given.

Growing plants actively draw nutrients from the soil in which they are planted. The believer who exercises his or her spiritual gifts constantly draws fresh nutrients from the spiritual soil, and those nutrients form the building blocks of putting on foliage and bearing more fruit. The sum total of our personal relationship with Christ, plus our God-given circumstances, resources, talents and network of relationships, are to be deployed in serving King Jesus. Grace blossoms and bears fruit in the doing of Kingdom work.

What is your spiritual gift? What are you doing to identify it, to put it into practice, to 'fan into flame the gift of God, which is in you' (2 Tim. 1:6)? This word picture is of a woodsman who builds a small pile of tinder, puts a spark to it, then fans it and blows on it, until it smolders and grows into flame. Don't neglect your gift, but put it to work until the master returns or calls you home. Devote yourself to speaking words of life or serving others, refining your skills, looking for needs, relying on the Spirit, bearing fruit in every good work.

HOW'S IT GOING?

Every farmer should occasionally pause from his labor, ride around his fields, and assess his operation critically. I call this 'management by driving around.' How are the crops? How can I do things more efficiently or effectively? To be honest, my farm never gets to where I aspire it to be.

So it is in the spiritual realm. We are called to imitate Christ, and to be perfect as our Father is perfect. But, how well are we actually doing in all our relationships? What if our spiritual walk is inconsistent, with frequent setbacks and sidetracks? That means we are like 100% of all believers! The Apostle Paul said about his own life, 'I delight in the law of God, in my inner being, but I see in my members another law waging war against the law of my mind and making me captive to the law of sin that dwells in my members. Wretched man that I am!' (Rom. 7:22-23). John Newton put it this way:

Neither our state [of righteousness] nor his honor are affected by the workings of indwelling sin, in the hearts of those whom he has taught to wrestle, strive, and mourn, on account of what they feel. Though sin wars, it shall not reign; and though it breaks our peace, it cannot separate from his love ... They are accepted in the Beloved, they have an Advocate with the Father, who once made an atonement for their sins, and ever lives to make intercession for their persons.[2]

What if I don't feel like I am living the victorious Christian life? Don't catastrophize! First, faith is not about feelings but about the reality of whether we trust Christ alone for our salvation. His all-sufficient grace is what our faith rests upon, not the degree of spiritual maturity we have achieved. Second, there is no such thing as the victorious Christian life, if by that we mean a life free of temptations and failures. The question is not whether sin remains in us, but whether we remain in our sin when we fail. Confess it, and keep walking with Christ. 'The righteous falls seven times, and rises again' (Prov. 24:16). Keep short accounts with God, confessing sin quickly when you stumble.

Humility to confess sin is the tap root of grace. 'God opposes the proud, but gives grace to the humble' (James 4:6). The secret of the Christian life is to keep walking humbly with God, relying on His grace and mercy, rather than trusting my own righteousness. Maintain a gospel balance between hope and despair. I despair of my sin, but rejoice and hope in my Savior: 'Let us then with confidence draw near to the throne of grace, that we may receive mercy and find grace to help in time of need' (Heb. 4:16). God knows our frame, and is always mindful that we are but dust.

At the end of the day, how do we *know* if we belong to God? Satan will accuse us of being such miserable sinners that God

---

2. *Select Letters*, p. 150.

could not possibly forgive us or love us. But do you cry out to 'Father' in times of temptation, fear, doubt, or failure? Only the Spirit of adoption can lead us to appeal to God as our Father. Do we lean on Christ more and more, looking to Him alone for all our needs, rather than relying on our own (insufficient) strength? If these things are so, we can know with assurance that we belong to God, and we will grow in grace, bearing fruit for His glory.

In biblical terminology, fruit means the end result. All who are called by His grace will bear fruit (Rom. 7:4). Joseph, the impetuous and foolish youth, grew into a wise, patient provider and protector for all Israel. Moses, a murderer and man on the run, transformed into the obedient law-giver and fearless prophet of God before Pharaoh. Paul, the self-righteous, legalistic hater of Christ's followers, became the chief apologist for the grace of God. Christ's promise is fail-proof: 'Whoever abides in me, and I in him, he it is that bears much fruit.'

So, back to the illustration of authenticated wine. How do I know if Christ is in me? Do I know, trust, and take comfort in His promises? Do I love God, and enjoy Him as my heavenly Father? Do I love to worship and praise Him? Do I abide in His Word? Do I love and serve His people? If so, true fruit is emerging. And it is ripening for His glory.

Grace always bears fruit.

8

THE HARVEST

'What is sown is perishable; what is raised is imperishable
.... for this mortal body must put on immortality'
(1 Cor. 15:42, 53).

In viticulture, the climax of the growing season is the harvest, commonly known as the 'crush.' After months of slow development, the final hours on the vine bring a spike in the sugar content of the grapes, which must be gathered and pressed at their peak. Plucked too soon, the grapes are not sweet enough to make the best wine. Delayed too long, the fruit begins to spoil. Carefully monitored, the hour – literally – comes when the fruit is ready, and teams of harvesters leap into action.

The harvest is anything but a sorrowful end of the growing season. It is a jubilant celebration, the culmination toward which all prior labors were devoted. Grapes fulfill their intended purpose when transformed into wine. And without the crush, there would be no wine.

So it is with our souls. Grace yields glory when we are transformed into eternal life. Without the harvest, there would be no glory. By grace, death is: (i) a reality to be faced; (ii) accompanied by special grace for the believer; (iii) a transition to new life; and (iv) a transformation into glory.

A REALITY TO BE FACED

When our son, Bryan, was about six years old, my father-in-law bought a new pickup truck. The first time Bryan climbed into the cab between his grandfather and me, he rubbed his little hands admiringly across the rich, leather seats and said, 'Pawpaw, when you die, will you leave this truck to me and my daddy?' Words cannot express the icy glare Jim shot in my direction.

'When you die.' Though we live in a time somewhat isolated from death as a daily threat, it is an ultimate reality for every human to face. The Book of Ecclesiastes teaches that there is a season for everything, 'a time to be born, and a time to die' (Eccles. 3:2). Though better standards of living and modern health care have stretched life expectancies to unprecedented lengths in human history, all flesh eventually fails. And, when it does, we all will reap what we have sown.

Which is why the 'Preacher' of Ecclesiastes says it is better to go to a funeral than a party, 'for this is the end of all mankind, and the living will lay it to heart … The heart of the wise is in the house of mourning, but the heart of fools is in the house of mirth' (Eccles. 7:2, 4). To 'lay it to heart' means to pay attention, and be ready. Like chopping and stacking firewood before winter, do not be caught off guard by a sudden change in the weather.

Our ability to lay it to heart fundamentally changes the way we live our life. The one who rejects the Creator, refusing to honor and thank Him, ought to eat, drink and be merry, for this temporal world is the best life has to offer. The believer, on the other hand, lives life facing (and embracing) eternity, and therefore both life and death are transformed by grace. Moses, though he lived to the ripe, old age of 120 years and was strong and vigorous to the end (Deut. 34:7), lived every day with an eye on eternity. His constant prayer was, 'So teach us to number our days, that we may get a heart of wisdom' (Ps. 90:12).

Psalm 49 also addresses the reality of death head-on: 'Man in his pomp will not endure; he is like the beasts that perish ... But God will redeem my soul from the power of Sheol; for he will receive me' (Ps. 49:12, 15 NASB).

The application for non-believers is simple: repent! Throw yourself on God's grace, and your plea for mercy will not be ignored. 'If we confess our sins, He is faithful and just to forgive us our sins, and to cleanse us from all unrighteousness' (1 John 1:9). The application for believers is to stay focused on the things that are above, where Christ is. Anticipating the destination transforms and enhances the journey.

ACCOMPANIED BY SPECIAL GRACE FOR THE BELIEVER

Andrew Rivet was a French pastor and theologian. On Christmas day in 1650, when he was seventy-seven years old, he preached a sermon but immediately thereafter took ill. He died on January 7, 1651, but not before recording these helpful words of prayer in his journal:

> The sense of divine favor increases in me every moment. My pains are tolerable, and my joys inestimable. I am no more vexed with earthly cares. I remember when any new book came out, how earnestly I have longed after it – but now all that is but dust. You are my all, O Lord; my good is to

approach to you. O what a library I have in God, in whom are all the treasures of wisdom and knowledge! You are the teacher of spirits – I have learned more divinity in these ten days that you have come to visit me, than I did in fifty years before.[1]

Dying grace is the special help the Lord gives His children as they pass from this life into the next. 'Precious in the eyes of the LORD is the death of his saints' (Ps. 116:15). The Lord promises to stay by our side when we pass through the valley of the shadow of death.

Robert Dabney, the Southern Presbyterian pastor and Confederate Army chaplain, who served as the aide-de-camp to General Stonewall Jackson, put it this way: 'Then it is that Jesus Christ draws near as an omnipotent Savior. He alone of all the universe has fathomed the deepest abysses of death, has explored all its caverns of despair, and has returned from them a conqueror … When our last hour comes, then let us say, brethren, "Lord Jesus, receive my spirit."'[2] Grace will come when grace is needed; ask for faith to outshine the dread of death.

John Newton understood well that salvation is by grace alone, from start to finish. He wrote a prayer many years before his death, which is helpful: 'Oh for grace to meet the approach of death with a humble, thankful, resigned spirit becoming my profession (of faith). That I may … be prepared and permitted to depart in peace and hope and be enabled, if I can speak, to bear my testimony to thy faithfulness and goodness with my last breath.'[3]

Newton wrote hymns for his nearly-illiterate congregation of farmers, blacksmiths, and laborers in Olney, England, using

---

1. Nancy Guthrie, *O Love That Will Not Let Me Go*, Crossway, 2011, p. 27.
2. Quoted in Ibid., p. 141.
3. Jonathan Aitken, *John Newton: From Disgrace to Grace,* p. 345.

simple words and steady meter to drive home biblical truths. One of his most enduring songs, published in the Olney Hymns in 1779, was 'The Lord Will Provide,' which boldly encourages us:

> When life sinks apace and death is in view,
> This word of his grace shall comfort us through:
> No fearing or doubting with Christ on our side,
> We hope to die shouting, 'The Lord will provide.'

Newton's prayer was answered. When a friend visited Newton during his final days in December 1807, and asked John how he was doing, he replied, 'My memory is nearly gone, but I remember two things: that I am a great sinner and that Christ is a great Savior.'[4] Following in his footsteps, we too can sing the closing words of his best-known hymn from the Olney Hymns, 'Amazing Grace:' 'Yes, when this flesh and heart shall fail, and mortal life shall cease, I shall possess, within the veil, a life of joy and peace.'

Douglas MacMillan, a Scottish pastor and former shepherd, wrote a book on Psalm 23, 'The Lord Our Shepherd.' In it, he recounts the testimony of his own father a few hours before he died: 'For forty years I have followed Christ, and for forty years I have prayed for grace to live for Christ, and for forty years I have prayed for grace to die like a Christian. I have always been afraid secretly – never admitted it, but I have always secretly been afraid that I wouldn't get grace to die. But now I see how stupid I was. God wouldn't give me grace I didn't need until I needed it; and when I need it, I have it. Don't be afraid of death, it's going to be wonderful.'[5]

---

4. Ibid., p. 347.

5. Douglas MacMillan, The Lord Our Shepherd, Bryntirion Press, 2003, p. 108.

The narrative of Stephen's death in Acts 7 vividly illustrates the way Christ walks closely with His people in their hour of death. Stephen 'gazed into heaven and saw the glory of God, and Jesus standing at the right hand of God. And he said, "Behold, I see the heavens opened, and the Son of Man standing at the right hand of God" … And as they were stoning Stephen, he called out, "Lord Jesus, receive my spirit" … And when he had said this, he fell asleep' (Acts 7:55, 59, 60).

Never let yourself believe for a moment that Psalm 23 has stopped working! 'Even though I walk through the valley of the shadow of death, I will fear no evil, for you are with me.' Then, more than ever, grace will carry us. Surely goodness and mercy, God's twin sheep dogs, will follow you all the days of your life, and you will dwell in the house of the Lord forever.

A TRANSITION TO NEW LIFE

There are several Hebrew words for death, including the basic concept of ceasing to breathe. But interestingly, there are two Hebrew idioms or expressions which affirm the steadfast truth that there is life beyond the grave. *'He slept with his fathers'* is covenant language, used to describe the deaths of Israel's kings, including David (1 Kings 2:10), Solomon (1 Kings 11:43), Rehoboam (1 Kings 14:31), Abijam (1 Kings 15:8), Asa (1 Kings 15:24), and many others. The phrase literally means 'to lie down,' or to rest from one's labors. The emphasis on peaceful sleep or rest carries over to the New Testament, where Paul says, 'But in fact Christ has been raised from the dead, the firstfruits of those who have fallen asleep … For as in Adam all die, so also in Christ shall all be made alive' (1 Cor. 15:20, 22). Or, again, 'There remains a Sabbath rest for the people of God, for whoever has entered God's rest has also rested from his works' (Heb. 4:9-10).

The other Hebrew expression for death is *gathered to his people,* as in, 'Abraham breathed his last and died in a good old age, an old man and full of years, and was gathered to his people' (Gen. 25:8). The same was said of Isaac (Gen. 35:29), Jacob (Gen. 49:33), Aaron (Num. 20:26), and Moses (Deut. 32:50). The emphasis here is on a joyful reunion. There is a family gathering on the other side, and therefore we have no reason to fear the transition.

Every Thanksgiving for the past thirty-five years or more, my wife's family has celebrated a reunion at Limerick. As many as 175 aunts, uncles, and cousins, with their spouses (the 'outlaws') and their children gather for a patriotic worship service, hay rides, outdoor games, and, of course, barbeque. The togetherness lasts all day, ending well after dusk around the campfire. Hugs, laughter, photographs, and memories flow freely. When asked what we do at Thanksgiving, Cathy's Aunt Deedie used to say, 'We just sit around admiring each other!' *That* is what it means to be gathered to one's people.

Who wouldn't look forward to a joyful reunion with our grandparents, parents, spouses, siblings, and children who have passed on before us? There was a common expression among cowboys in the old West, 'throw your hat across the creek.' Those words are carved into the mantle in the lodge at the A-Bar-A Ranch in Encampment, Wyoming, to this day. You see, the cowboy's hat was his single most important piece of equipment. It sheltered him from the sun, protected him from the cold or rain, and doubled as a canteen for water or a feed bucket for his horse. Therefore, to throw his hat across the creek meant to irrevocably commit to a course of action. Once the hat is on the other side, there is no turning back. In the same way, the believer is called to live and die with a forward-looking, no-turning-back mindset.

The resounding message of God's Word, from start to finish, is that death is not an ending, but a transformation to eternal life. To be absent from the body is to be present with the Lord.

TRANSFORMED INTO GLORY

In 1 Corinthians 15, Paul uses agricultural imagery to explain how our earthly body will be transformed into a heavenly body. 'There are heavenly bodies and earthly bodies, but the glory of the heavenly is of one kind, and the glory of the earthly is of another ... So it is with the resurrection of the dead. What is sown is perishable; what is raised is imperishable. It is sown in dishonor, it is raised in glory. It is sown in weakness; it is raised in power. It is sown a natural body, it is raised a spiritual body' (1 Cor. 15: 40, 42-44). The features which marked our natural body – weakness, temporariness, and shame – will give way to a new image, one of power, permanence, and glory. 'Death is swallowed up in victory ... through our Lord Jesus Christ' (v. 54, 56).

Death is the final tran-sition of our earthly sanctification. Paul assures us that glory awaits all who are in Christ: 'But our citi-zenship is in heaven, and from it we await a Savior, the Lord Jesus Christ, who will trans-form our lowly body to be like his glorious body, by the power that enables him to subject all things to

himself' (Phil. 3:20-21). He boldly proclaims, 'And I am sure of this, that he who began a good work in you will bring it to completion at the day of Christ Jesus' (Phil. 1:6).

This is a sweet promise, to be enjoyed both now and when we come near death's gate. 'The blessed Holy Spirit has already sealed it to my soul with rich and full comfort ... Do not let this song lie on the shelf until your last day. Sing it all the days of your life.'[6]

The day of our death is the day we will be transported from the kingdom of grace to the kingdom of glory. The battle will be over, and we will enter our rest. Christ's kingdom is rooted in this world, but spreads its limbs and bears its fruit in the world to come.

Will you be ready for the harvest? Grace will bring you all the way home.

6. C. H. Spurgeon, *Beside Still Waters,* Thomas Nelson Publishers, 1999, p. 63.

9

THE FEAST

*'I tell you I will not drink again of this fruit of the vine
until that day when I drink it new with you in my Father's
kingdom' (Matt. 26:29).*

Harvest festivals have been an integral part of the winemaking
tradition for centuries, in the Middle East, Europe, and in the
New World. Celebrating the culmination of many months
of painstaking labor, the local festivals are always exuberant
occasions, showcasing the heart and soul of winemaking.

One of the most colorful and historic festivals occurs
in St. Emilion, a beautiful village in the Bordeaux region of
southwestern France. The elaborate celebration starts with
members of the local winemaking guild parading through the
village in scarlet robes to the village church to give thanks.
The days-long event includes large parades, marvelous feasts,
spectacular fireworks, and vibrant music and dancing, all in a
joyful mood. It is the village's big event of the year, not to be
missed.

Yet St. Emilion, in its quaint splendor, will pale in comparison to the feast of the Lamb, soon to occur in the new heavens and the new earth. It will be the biggest, loudest, greatest celebration of all eternity, and you don't want to miss it. The consummation of the covenant of grace will be celebrated royally at the marriage supper of the Lamb: 'Then I heard what seemed to be the voice of a great multitude, like the roar of many waters and like the sound of mighty peals of thunder, crying out, "Hallelujah! For the Lord our God the Almighty reigns. Let us rejoice and exult and give him the glory, for the marriage of the Lamb has come ... Blessed are those who are invited to the marriage supper of the Lamb"' (Rev. 19:6-7, 9). Notice the vivid details given by John, describing the atmosphere and the attire of the wedding party: there will be (i) shouts of joy, (ii) by countless multitudes clothed in righteousness, and (iii) with absolute certainty.

CRIES OF REJOICING

The Apostle John's vision of the risen, victorious Jesus Christ and 'the things that must soon take place' is recorded in the Book of Revelation, to comfort and assure His servants (Rev. 1:1). After describing the events which will take place in the last days, including the promised return of Christ, the final defeat of Satan, the destruction of the world as we know it, the general resurrection and judgment of all mankind, and the unveiling of the new heavens and the new earth, John describes a great celebration which will take place. Human language and life experience failed to adequately express the glory and power and magnificence of the occasion, but that did not stop John from trying. Listen again to his words: 'Then I heard what *seemed* to be the voice of a great multitude, *like* the roar of many waters and *like* the sound of mighty peals of thunder, crying out,

"Hallelujah! For the Lord our God the Almighty reigns. Let us rejoice and exult and give him the glory."' Like a spontaneous victory shout from an army, like the roar of a great waterfall, like the crash of lightning and the peals of thunder, all rolled into one. Like, like, like. The victory cry will be deafening!

What phrase will the multitudes be shouting? 'Hallelujah!' (Rev. 19:1, 3, 4, and 6). This exuberant expression echoes the refrain of Psalms 146-150 (though most English translations render it, 'Praise the LORD!'). Taken from Hebrew, it is an imperative to 'praise Jah' or 'praise Jehovah,' an adoring, exultant exclamation of love and worship.

On Christmas Eve in 2019, the well-practiced choir and a full orchestra at First Presbyterian Church in Columbia performed Glenn Rudolph's anthem, 'The Dream Isaiah Saw,' whose final stanza thunders with full voice, full organ, full brass, and full percussion. When the conductor suddenly drew the climactic crescendo to silence, the congregation sat in a prolonged, stunned silence. In the back of the sanctuary, a small boy could be heard exclaiming, 'Wowwww!' There is no better way to express the joy and magnitude of the thundering cries that will ring out at the feast of the Lamb.

Every week on the Lord's Day, we are granted an opportunity to practice our praises for the great feast. Think of each Lord's Day as a dress rehearsal for the coming celebration. Ask the Lord for the Spirit's help to learn, practice and love the songs and the shouts of rejoicing.

CLOTHED IN RIGHTEOUSNESS

At a wedding, almost universally, the importance and joy of the occasion is marked by the special garb of the wedding party. The bridesmaids and groomsmen wear gowns, tuxedos, or other sartorial flourishes to set them apart from the guests.

But the greatest honor is reserved for the bride, who wears an exquisite gown, a long train, a special veil, or carries a fancy bouquet to properly place her at the center of attention. And so it will be at the feast of the Lamb. 'His Bride has made herself ready; it was granted her to clothe herself with fine linen, bright and pure – for the fine linen is the righteous deeds of the saints' (Rev. 19:7-8).

This, too, is a gift of grace. The immeasurable riches of our Father include giving us the very wedding garb we will wear to the feast! 'For we are his workmanship, created in Christ Jesus for good works, which God prepared beforehand, that we should walk in them' (Eph. 2:10). Though the deeds themselves are the products of His grace, they will fit us appropriately. Any act, as simple as a cup of cold water offered to a brother or sister in need, will be remembered and celebrated. If I can put it this way, the garments of righteousness will fit us well, because they were specifically tailored for us. The Lord equips us His people with unique gifts, opportunities, and relationships, through which His grace is displayed, and which will be recounted and celebrated.

It is not the dramatic things alone, but also the routine things, which will be celebrated. A word of Christian witness or a word of encouragement spoken to another. A shared meal, a financial gift or a common act of assistance. Perhaps one of the 'gracest' (greatest graces) is an act of reconciliation, where an offender or an offended reaches out to the other party to make peace. 'A harvest of righteousness is sown in peace by those who make peace' (James 3:18).

Ask for the Spirit's help to do relationships right. A faithful spouse, a loving and gentle parent, a loyal employee, a fair boss, an obedient child – the angels in heaven watch breathlessly to see such displays of beauty and grace. These things will be remembered and celebrated at the feast. Like wedding guests telling anecdotes and offering toasts at a rehearsal dinner, so the stories of grace will be re-told over and over, to cheers and rejoicing.

CERTAIN RELIABILITY

The marriage feast of the Lamb is not a sentimental, hoped-for view of what heaven will be like. It's a certain reality. The angel said to the Apostle John, 'Write this: Blessed are those who are invited to the marriage supper of the Lamb.' And he said to me, 'These are the true words of God' (Rev. 19:9). Notice the double emphasis: write these words down; they are true.

When God says someone is 'blessed,' that is not wishful sentiment, but a categorical statement of fact. The one on whom He pronounces a blessing *is* blessed indeed. The great theologian, John Owen, understood the connection between the future reality and the present circumstances of our lives: 'if our future blessedness shall consist in being where he is, and beholding of his glory, what better preparation can there be for it than in ... contemplation of that glory ... unto this very end, that by a view of it we may be transformed into the same glory?'[1] In other words, there is a gracious link between the future celebration of Christ's marriage in glory and the current struggles of life: 'For contemplation of the glory of Christ will carry us cheerfully, comfortably, and victoriously through life and death, and all that we have to conflict withal in either of them.'[2]

Jesus, the man full of grace and truth, constantly emphasized the eternal security of His people. He spoke of this on the last night He was with His disciples, celebrating the Passover in

---

1. Sinclair Ferguson, *John Owen on the Christian Life,* The Banner of Truth Trust, 1987, p. 279.

2. Ibid., p. 278.

the Upper Room. 'In my Father's house are many rooms. If it were not so, would I have told you that I go to prepare a place for you? And if I go and prepare a place for you, I will come again and will take you to myself, that where I am you may be also' (John 14:2-3). Ask for the help of the Spirit to start contemplating the glory of Christ and the blessing of being on His guest list! And not merely as a guest, but rather as the bride! In a wonderful and mysterious way, the church as a whole will be the beloved bride of the King. May God give us grace to be ready for that sure and great day.

Grace will celebrate a great feast.

AFTERWORD

Let's go back to that vineyard at Limerick, say, in late August.

As the afternoon shadows grow long, the distinct, high-pitched drone of cicadas rises from the pine woods. The summer eve is oppressively hot and humid. But something about the golden hue of the vineyard feels promising. Cooler days are near.

In the vineyard, fat clusters of muscadines and scuppernongs hang from lush vines. The rich purple and bronze colors signal ripeness, and a soft squeeze confirms it. A quick 'field test' bursts with sweet, mellow flavor. Time to harvest! Hands move quickly – but gently – among the vines, gathering the clusters of succulent fruit.

Harvest caps off months of patient labor. Prune in winter, cultivate in spring, tend in summer, harvest in fall. Each progressive season in viticulture brings slow, steady growth, with a surge of ripening at the end. It's a rhythmical cycle, a beautiful drama, this fruit-bearing of the vine.

In the same, amazing way, the seasons of life slowly unfold for the believer. Each brings new blessings and challenges. But the fruit of His grace at every stage will remain on display for all eternity. Christ is in you, the hope of glory.

It is hard to capture grace more fully than songwriter Michael Perry did in Cathy's favorite hymn, *O God Beyond All Praising*:

> *O God beyond all praising, we worship you today*
> *And sing the love amazing that songs cannot re-pay;*
> *For we can only wonder at every gift you send,*
> *At blessings without number and mercies without end:*
> *We lift our hearts before you and wait upon your word,*
> *We honor and adore you, our great and mighty Lord.*
>
> *The flow'r of earthly splendor in time must surely die,*
> *Its fragile bloom surrender to you, the Lord most high;*
> *But hidden from all nature the eternal seed is sown,*
> *Though small in mortal stature, to heaven's garden grown;*
> *For Christ the man from heaven from death has set us free,*
> *And we through him are given the final victory.*
>
> *Then hear, O gracious Savior, accept the love we bring,*
> *That we who know your favor may serve you as our King;*
> *And whether our tomorrows be filled with good or ill,*
> *We'll triumph through our sorrows and rise to praise you still:*
> *To marvel at your beauty and glory in your ways,*
> *And make a joyful duty our sacrifice of praise.*

When the chill of fall arrives, the leaves have dropped, and the fruit is gone, one lasting reminder of God's goodness is left clinging to the arbor. The tendrils of His grace will *never* let you go!

Also available from Christian Focus Publications…

100 Devotional Readings
on Union With Christ

HOW TO LIVE AN
'IN CHRIST' LIFE

KENNETH BERDING

How to Live an 'In Christ' Life

100 Devotional Readings on Union with Christ

Kenneth Berding

- 'In Christ' phrases from New Testament
- Identity, life, community and mission
- 100 devotions

Everywhere we look in the letters of Paul we encounter 'in Christ.' But how many of us know why the Apostle Paul uses this expression—or ones like it—over and over again in his letters? What is so important about being in Christ? Is it possible that when Paul talks about *inChristness*, he is handing us a set of keys that will open up his letters and reveal what is most essential to living the Christian life? In these 100 devotional readings, we discover why *inChristness* is so important and how to live an in–Christ life.

ISBN: 978-1-5271-0559-1

IX 9Marks | First Steps Series

CHARACTER

HOW DO I CHANGE?

SHARON DICKENS

SERIES EDITED BY MEZ McCONNELL

Character

How Do I Change?

Sharon Dickens

- Part of the First Steps series
- For new Christians
- How to grow in godliness

So, you've heard the Gospel, you've accepted Jesus as your saviour, you're going to Church regularly – you're definitely a Christian, but you don't feel like you're acting like one. The other Christians you know all seem to have it together but how do you get to that point? Even though none of us will be perfect in this life, we can grow to be more and more like Jesus. This book will tell you how.

ISBN: 978-1-5271-0101-2

KINGDOM CITIZENSHIP

KRIS BROSSETT

UNDERSTANDING GOD, HIS PLAN, AND OUR PLACE IN IT.

Kingdom Citizenship

Understanding God, His Plan, and Our Place in it

Kris Brossett

- 6–Week Study
- Brokenness, Promise, Grace, Sanctification, Church & Christian Walk

Everyone grows up, but maturity is a choice. In the same way, becoming a mature Christian requires a choice to actively pursue spiritual growth. It's important to learn what the Bible teaches about God and to obey what you learn. Whether you're a new Christian, you've been a Christian for a long time, or you're interested in Christianity, this six–week study will help you to know God, to live boldly for Him, and to grow into Christian maturity.

ISBN: 978-1-5271-0410-5

Christian Focus Publications

Our mission statement –

STAYING FAITHFUL

In dependence upon God we seek to impact the world through literature faithful to His infallible Word, the Bible. Our aim is to ensure that the Lord Jesus Christ is presented as the only hope to obtain forgiveness of sin, live a useful life and look forward to heaven with Him.

Our Books are published in four imprints:

CHRISTIAN
FOCUS

popular works including biographies, commentaries, basic doctrine and Christian living.

CHRISTIAN
HERITAGE

books representing some of the best material from the rich heritage of the church.

MENTOR

books written at a level suitable for Bible College and seminary students, pastors, and other serious readers. The imprint includes commentaries, doctrinal studies, examination of current issues and church history.

CF4•K

children's books for quality Bible teaching and for all age groups: Sunday school curriculum, puzzle and activity books; personal and family devotional titles, biographies and inspirational stories – Because you are never too young to know Jesus!

Christian Focus Publications Ltd,
Geanies House, Fearn, Ross-shire,
IV20 1TW, Scotland, United Kingdom.
www.christianfocus.com